Alma M. Wagner

293 Longcommon Rd.
Riverside, Ill

BEETHOVEN
AND THE WORLD OF MUSIC

Also by Manuel Komroff

ABRAHAM LINCOLN

MOZART

NAPOLEON

TRUE ADVENTURES OF SPIES

JULIUS CAESAR

MARCO POLO

Beethoven

AND THE WORLD OF MUSIC

BY

Manuel Komroff

DODD, MEAD & COMPANY

NEW YORK, 1961

ACKNOWLEDGMENTS

The author and publisher wish to thank the following for their generous permission to quote from their books:

Alfred A. Knopf, Inc., for the extracts from *Beethoven: His Spiritual Development* by John W. N. Sullivan.

Random House, Inc., for the quotations from *The Life and Works of Beethoven* by John N. Burk.

Holt, Rinehart and Winston, Inc., for the lines from *Beethoven: The Man Who Freed Music* by Robert Haven Schauffler.

The text of the Heiligenstadt Testament and of the letter by Bettina Brentano are reprinted from *Beethoven: Letters, Journals and Conversations,* edited, translated and introduced by Michael Hamburger and published by Pantheon Books.

CONTENTS

1. Of time, liberty and birth   1
2. Youth   9
3. Vienna   28
4. Love of the three countesses   42
5. The enigma of the immortal
   beloved   47
6. The world of sound grows dim   52
7. Eroica   63
8. A sheaf of masterpieces   69
9. Within the furnace of creation   84
10. The man   88
11. Beethoven and goethe   101
12. End of a period   115
13. Karl   130

14. JOURNEY INTO A NEW WORLD   138

15. LAST DAYS AND LAST WORDS   159

   Selected Bibliography   173

   Selected List of Beethoven Music and Recordings   175

   Index   179

1

OF TIME, LIBERTY AND BIRTH

BEETHOVEN was born at a time when society was undergoing an important transformation, a change that ushered in our world of today. Ideas of equality and liberty were in the air. The ancient and medieval notion of a society built on aristocracy with a ruling privileged class was seriously questioned. Yet, while feudalism was already dead, its skeleton still stalked about.

The slow inroads of reason soon gave way to violence. Beethoven was five and a half years old when the war for American independence began. And although America was far from the Rhineland of his birth, still the Hessians and Hanoverians hired by the English king came from nearby provinces. The fever of freedom was aglow in the Rhineland as it was in many lands. But in France it suddenly broke out in a bloody revolution that shook the whole of Europe.

Beethoven was nineteen when the Bastille fell. He was twenty-three when Marie Antoinette went to the guillotine. He was twenty-nine when, out of chaos, the victorious Na-

poleon became First Consul of the Republic of France, the
first great modern republic to be born in Europe. These were
all world-shaking events that left their mark on Beethoven's
mind.

But music by custom remained aloof. It considered itself
removed from politics. It saw no reason why it should reflect
the spirit of its time. Music makers were content to hold to
the traditional tonal discourses and toy with polite and agreeable sound. Although Beethoven, from his earliest compositions, displayed a different temper, a temper in which was
injected a note of dramatic individuality, he, too, in the beginning, held to the old forms. And he was slow in reflecting
the spirit of his time.

The definite breakthrough, and this was the moment he
raised music into a new realm, did not come until he was
thirty-four years old. It was in this year, 1804, that he composed his famous symphony No. 3, the *Eroica*. On the first
page of this epoch-making composition he wrote "composed
on the subject of Bonaparte." The symphony was dedicated
to Napoleon. But in this same year Napoleon crowned himself emperor, and Beethoven in anger scratched out the
dedication.

Then, instead of the hoped for and promised equality,
fraternity and liberty, Europe was torn by ten years of war.
The fumes were still in the air when the crowned heads of
Europe gathered at the Congress of Vienna. Here they cut
up the map of Europe and made a feeble attempt to restore
dead kingdoms and bring back the old frightened aristocracy,
on the theory that they alone were the appointed and "legiti-
mate" rulers over man. In this year Beethoven was forty-five.

It was during the Congress of Vienna that Beethoven had

the privilege of inviting to a concert, in his own name, all the sovereigns who were in Vienna. Beethoven was now famous. His music was famous. He considered himself the equal of anyone, titled or untitled. He was aware of his genius and he carried himself with pride. He faced the aristocracy, as he faced the world, a free man. All his life he had breathed in the air of equality and freedom. And his music was part of his life.

But it was a long time before he was able to relate the outer world to his inner world. It was many years before he could cast aside the established traditions and tonal platitudes of his day. But once he was free of the fetters of convention, he was able to plumb new emotional depths.

The general public was not ready for such a revolutionary change. The whole musical world was shaken. The shock was not unlike the impact of the French Revolution on the political world. But once the event had happened, it could not be thrown off. There was no going back to the old order.

Thus it is that life and art are closely bound together. Imagination lives and creates in the air that surrounds the artist. It takes life from this air. And more: the air that gives it life also gives it character.

The nineteenth century began with a call for liberation. This century marks the emergence of the common man. To this dramatic stage, from deep obscurity, came the inspired genius of Beethoven. It was in this political climate that he spent his youth, dreamed the dreams of aspiration and, by passionate integrity, slowly came into the full bloom of his creative maturity. The force of his creative imagination took its vitality from the new freedom which was born in his time.

It all began in 1770. In this year Marie Antoinette left her home in Vienna to marry the heir to the throne of France. Mozart in this year was fourteen years old and already famous throughout Europe. Both Handel and the great J. S. Bach were already dead. But Bach's son, Karl Philipp Emanuel, who had done so much for keyboard music and established the sonata form, was still alive. Karl Philipp Emanuel Bach greatly influenced Franz Joseph Haydn who, in this year of 1770, was thirty-eight years old.

In December of this year, 1770, Beethoven was born in the little town of Bonn, about twenty miles south of Cologne, on the west bank of the river Rhine.

It was to this town of Bonn that Beethoven's grandfather had come, thirty-seven years before, to be court musician to the Elector of Cologne at a salary of 400 florins. The van Beethovens were a Flemish family and the name is still to be found in Holland and Belgium. But unlike the *von* in German the Flemish *van* implies no mark of aristocracy.

The grandfather was born in Flanders and he was once said to have been the son of a master tailor. But recent research has proved that he was the son of a baker who, in later life, became a dealer in lace. There is also a story in circulation that the Cologne Elector, the Archbishop Clemens August, heard a twenty-one-year-old church singer in Louvain, or possibly Liége, who had a pleasing voice and good musical knowledge and so the Elector invited him to enter his service. This was young Ludwig van Beethoven, who later became the grandfather of Beethoven. He migrated to Bonn in 1733.

The Archbishop Elector who had brought this singer from

Flanders was a true prince of the eighteenth century. He had extravagant ideas; he was worldly; he traveled; he loved good music, art and women, He loved good food, wine, opera and drama. He had a talent for raising money and a passion for spending it. Under his rule Bonn grew architecturally. He was guardian and mentor of its culture. With "crook and scepter" he ruled over his pocket-handkerchief monarchy.

Bonn has an old history. In ancient times it was a Roman military settlement. But it was twice destroyed: once by barbarians and a second time in 889 by bands of Norse raiders who sailed the river Rhine. Ever since the year 1265 the Electors of Cologne had made their residence in Bonn. At the time Beethoven was born the city had a population of 10,000.

Beethoven lived to see his birthplace conquered by the French and he lived to see his Rhineland country joined to Prussia by the Congress of Vienna.

Soon after coming to Bonn, the young Ludwig van Beethoven, feeling secure in the service of the Elector, married a young woman named Maria. To augment his income, and since the town was surrounded by rich vineyards, he went into the wine business as a side line. In the palace, where he served as organist and choir singer, he soon rose to positions of responsibility which, as the years wore on, gave him the rank of *Kapellmeister,* or Master of the court orchestra. Of the three children born to the van Beethovens, two died in infancy, but the third, a boy named Johann, survived.

The boy's mother, Maria, left alone among the wine barrels, became a hopeless alcoholic, and was boarded during her last years in a Bonn convent. Johann, who was destined to become Beethoven's father, also took to heavy drinking when he grew to manhood.

In time the old Elector died and when the new Elector Max came to the palace in Bonn he found two Beethovens in his employ. Beethoven the *Kapellmeister* was then forty-nine, and his son Johann, to whom he had taught the rudiments of instrumental music and choir singing, was twenty-one. But the youth, who was handsome and very vain, never acquired any of his father's musical artistry. From the start, and to the end of his days, he was a mediocre musician. At first he was tolerated because of his father. When the *Kapellmeister* died, Johann was kept on only because of his many years of service.

When Johann was twenty-seven he fell in love with a young woman of twenty-one, Maria Magdalena Laym. Her father, who was now dead, had been chief cook in a nearby castle. She had been married for a short time to a court valet, but he too had died.

Johann's father objected to his son's marriage because he thought the girl was of lower station. In his eyes the daughter of a cook was lower than the son of a *Kapellmeister*, even though both the cook and the musician were servants in the court. But Johann brushed his father's objections aside and the marriage took place.

Maria van Beethoven was a quiet girl, gentle, hard-working, amiable, tactful and sad, very sad. A neighbor has recorded that Maria was never known to laugh. As the wife of a good-looking, shallow, uneducated and mediocre singer she had little joy in life. Often Johann came home drunk, having spent his last money in the tavern.

Keeping the home together, cleaning, washing, cooking, paying the rent and bills for food, repairing the clothes—— everything fell on her frail shoulders. In twelve years she was pregnant six times, but only three of the children survived.

Her eyes were sad, her face serious. The weight of life was heavy. She once said to her neighbor, "What is marriage? A little joy, followed by a chain of sorrows." And she dragged this long heavy chain of interlinking sorrows with her to the brink of her grave.

This was the mother of the composer Beethoven.

The first of Maria's children to survive was named Ludwig in honor of his grandfather, the *Kapellmeister* of the Elector's orchestra. It was customary in Catholic Bonn to christen an infant the day after birth. The church register records the date as December 17, 1770. And so it is assumed that Ludwig van Beethoven was born on the sixteenth of December, 1770.

Grandpa Ludwig loved his little grandson, and the child clung to the old man with devoted affection. But on Christmas Eve, 1773, when Little Ludwig was three years old, the old man died.

Later two more sons were born to Johann and Maria van Beethoven. They were named Karl and Johann. Ludwig, the first born, was four years older than Karl and six years older than Johann.

After the death of the good *Kapellmeister* the family fortunes began to sink. The child looked on. He saw his silent, sad mother working desperately to hold the wretched home together. He was ashamed of his drunken father and was weighed down by the poverty that surrounded them. He, too, became silent and his eyes reflected a deep inner sadness. They looked out but they did not see. A brooding nature soon took possession of him. And all his life long it remained with him.

2

YOUTH

BEING a man with a compelling weakness, which he displayed publicly in the little town of Bonn, and having failed to attain his late father's position as *Kapellmeister*—although he did petition the Elector—Johann took revenge on his children. A neighbor has recorded that "the Beethoven children were not brought up with kindness; they were often left to servants. The father was very severe with them." When company was expected, the boys, because they were considered boisterous and ill-mannered, were sent out of the house. Their parents, either through ignorance or indifference, never instructed the children in social graces. This early neglect was to show up years later in many little ways. Unintentional bad manners and a complete disregard for social amenities were to prove a handicap to Beethoven, who was dependent on society for patronage.

Since music was the business of the family, Johann began teaching Ludwig at an early age. The boy took easily to both the violin and pianoforte. He was quick to learn. The father, aware of the profit that could come from a talented child, lost no time. Did not little Mozart play before the crowned heads of Europe? Here was a rare opportunity. Here was an easy entrance to the glittering world of the aristocracy. Here waited fame, jeweled presents and money. When little Beethoven was five, Mozart was nineteen and a sensational musical wonder. Mozart's piano technique and his compositions were the talk of Europe. Already at nineteen Mozart had composed symphonies, concertos, chamber music, operas, and a hundred and fifty other compositions! He was world famous.

And so it was that the Mozart legend at that period penetrated and colored every musical home in Europe. A few years later Paganini, a brutal dock laborer in Genoa, Italy, beat his son and forced him to practice the violin, almost day and night, all because of Mozart's brilliant success. Hundreds of children in Europe, having but a tiny grain of musical talent, were flogged and brutalized. Beethoven also was beaten. But from so many, only a very few Beethovens and Paganinis emerged.

Neighbors have recorded that they often saw the young Ludwig standing on a stool before the clavier, weeping bitter tears. Johann beat his son and at times locked him in the cellar in order to make him obedient and develop his talent. If music did not inspire the boy, at least he could attain some technical proficiency by practice.

One of Johann's drinking companions, a tenor in the Elector's court and also a fair pianist, records that often late at night Beethoven's father, coming in from the wine house, would rouse the boy from his sleep and "keep him at the pianoforte until morning."

As for the other two boys, Karl and Johann, the father soon discovered that musically they were hopeless. And so, being stupid, they were spared the drudgery and the beatings.

As time progressed there were fewer beatings and the boy found the piano more agreeable. But instead of studying the scales he would let his fingers wander over the keyboard seeking combinations of rhythm and sound in improvisation. His father, who little understood his son, would lecture him about this and insist that he learn to play the written music before he played things out of his head.

The music lessons took first place. Beethoven attended a small public school and later a Latin school, but not for long. His general education was badly neglected. At fourteen he left school for good. Although he later was able to instruct himself in literature and to acquire a smattering of French and Italian through operas, his spelling was poor, and in arithmetic he could just manage addition. To the end of his days division and multiplication remained a mystery.

Most of the things he learned he picked up for himself. The ability to learn on his own was an important asset, and in time it became even more important. We will soon see that distinguished composers, like Joseph Haydn, and others, were unable to teach him the kind of musical composition he desired. But this knowledge he was able to acquire by himself.

When Beethoven was eight years old his father arranged a concert in Cologne for him, together with a young woman contralto. The local paper recorded that the young lady sang arias and the "little boy of six years old played clavier concertos and trios."

Here we see that Johann had taken two years off the boy's

age to make him seem more remarkable. When Mozart was young his father also lied about his son's age for the same reason. And since Ludwig was not a big boy for his age, he could easily pass for six. In fact, Johann continued with this false reckoning so long that Beethoven grew into manhood believing himself to be two years younger than he really was. Due to this, the entire Bonn chronology was confused, and only years later was it finally corrected and firmly established by Beethoven's distinguished biographer, Thayer.

We have no record of the compositions that the eight-year-old Beethoven played in Cologne at this, his first concert, beyond the words "concertos and trios." And there is no record to tell us if the concert was a success. It probably was not, for had it been, the ambitious father would surely have arranged another.

Johann now realized that Ludwig needed better instruction than he was capable of giving. Between the ages of eight and ten, or eleven, Beethoven had an odd assortment of instructors. First there was Tobias Pfeiffer, the Court Tenor who was Johann's drinking companion. But these lessons did not last very long. Then the old Court Organist, Van den Eeden, who was almost seventy, showed the boy the intricate mechanism of the organ. Ludwig tried the keys, but his legs were not long enough to reach the pedals.

It is recorded that the eager youth made friends with Friar Willibald Koch, the organist at the Franciscan monastery at Bonn. Also, he made friends with the organist of the Minorites Cloister, where he found the organ large and complicated; and with Zenser, the organist of the Münster church.

At this time of his youth Ludwig is described as being dark, with a mop of black hair and a complexion as swarthy as a Spaniard. He was short, stocky, shy, morose, with a thick neck and round nose. He was unclean and his clothes were neglected. He was not a happy youth. Yet there was something in him, his earnestness, his eagerness—something that inspired confidence and brushed his unattractiveness aside. He had a wonderful talent for making friends. This trait, already marked when he was only ten years old, remained with him all his life.

At the monastery and at the cloister he was soon allowed to play the organ for an occasional service. At the same time he continued his lessons with the old Court Organist, Van den Eeden, and he soon learned how to extend his short legs to reach the organ pedals. When on occasion he substituted for Van den Eeden, he would improvise his own preludes and stretch them out with variations and embellishments, to the great astonishment, and often annoyance, of the members of the orchestra.

So far his instruction had not been too methodical. Here and there he picked up what he could. But one day, by a stroke of good fortune, there arrived in Bonn a thoroughly trained and gifted musician. Christian Gottlob Neefe came to Bonn from Leipzig in the year 1779. He was a composer and a good organist, and possessed musical taste and imagination. This son of a tailor has been described as being "stoop-shouldered" and a "touching figure." Yet he was young, only thirty-one, and he possessed everything that the young Beethoven greatly needed.

From Leipzig, Neefe had brought with him some of the sonatas of Karl Philipp Emanuel Bach, whose fame at that time was much greater than that of his late father. Mozart had already played his compositions in concerts. It is of this

Karl Philipp Emanuel Bach that Mozart once said, "He is the father, we are the children." But what was more important, Neefe brought with him, in manuscript (the work was not printed until many years later), a copy of Johann Sebastian Bach's *The Well-tempered Clavier*. This work, now world renowned, consists of two volumes, each containing twenty-four preludes and fugues—one in each major and minor key.

Neefe soon recognized the boy's ability. He gave him the musical discipline and constructive criticism which he badly needed. And Neefe was more than pleased with his pupil's rapid progress and his ability to understand musical forms. "If he goes on as he has begun he will become a second Mozart," he said of Beethoven.

Impressed with his pupil's "forceful and finished" playing, as well as with his ability to read at sight, he lost no time in giving him Bach's *Well-tempered Clavier* as his major piano project. This is difficult music for a young boy but temperamentally Beethoven was well suited to it. He understood its brooding, musical tonalities. He liked its dramatic, inspirational and imaginative qualities.

Very soon, under the patient and capable Neefe, he began the mastery of these difficult preludes and fugues.

Beethoven's early training in Bach had a tremendous influence not only on his piano playing but also on his composition and on modern piano technique. He first made his fame in Vienna as a virtuoso by his masterly performance of the "Forty-eight." Later Beethoven instructed young Karl Czerny in these preludes and fugues. And when young Franz Liszt became the pupil of Czerny, this Bach piano discipline became part of his training. And in turn Liszt passed it on to his many pupils, the last of whom have only recently de-

parted this world. Certainly this long musical chain extends
through many generations. What Neefe started with young
Beethoven has traveled far, over many lands, and has greatly
influenced modern piano composition and technique.

"If I ever become a great man," Beethoven once wrote to
Neefe, "you shall have a share of the credit."

When Beethoven was twelve, the old Court Organist died
and the position was given to Neefe. The young Beethoven
became his assistant and played the organ during rehearsals
and at times when Neefe was otherwise occupied.

A year later Beethoven was officially recognized and made
"deputy cembalist" of the Elector's orchestra. (The cembal
was one of the forerunners of the piano.) He wore the
Elector's livery: bright red with heavy gold braid. And he
wore a small powdered wig. His duties were various. He
accompanied the singers and conducted the orchestra during
rehearsals. He set the tempo and kept them playing together.
He served as aid to the organist and helped the *Kapellmeister*.
Here was a position in which a young musician could experience and learn a great deal.

During this period and under the inspirational guidance of
his teacher, Neefe, Beethoven wrote his first composition:
Variations on a March by Dressler. He also composed three
piano sonatas which he proudly dedicated to the Elector.

All this time he had been serving as "deputy cembalist"
without pay. However, in February 1784, having reached the
mature age of fourteen, he sent a petition to the Elector for
official recognition, applying for the position of assistant
court organist.

Although the Elector approved of Beethoven's application,

he was at that moment short of funds and he delayed fixing a salary for Beethoven's services. In April the Elector died. But his throne was not empty long.

Empress Maria Theresa of Austria, who was also Queen of Hungary and Bohemia, had long had her eyes on Cologne. Her daughter Marie Antoinette was Queen of France, and her other daughter, Marie Caroline, was Queen of Naples. Her son Ferdinand she made ruler of Modena, a province in northern Italy. But her youngest son, the Archduke Maximilian Franz, was without a throne. This she felt was unfair. And so her greedy eyes had long scanned the map of Europe. Now at last there was a death and a vacancy. She acted fast.

In no time at all Maximilian Franz, the twenty-eight-year-old son of Maria Theresa, came to occupy the palace in Bonn. Maximilian was not an archbishop, but this lack of theological training was easily overcome. He retired to a seminary in Cologne and in three weeks became a fully consecrated priest. Although he was never a devoted man of the Church, he nevertheless made a good ruler. He was very fat, genial, informal, well educated in the arts and sciences. And he knew how to select good ministers. He and his family had long been devoted to music. His brother and his sisters all played instruments. He himself played the viola and is said to have had a fairly pleasing voice. He collected a large library of music. And besides music, Maximilian was also a patron of the arts and sciences. It was because of his efforts that the university, now famous, was established in Bonn. He also created a botanical garden and opened a free reading room in the palace library. In short, he brought with him to Bonn a sample of Viennese culture. He was destined to be the last of the Electors of Cologne.

Soon after his arrival he approved of young Beethoven's appointment and set his salary at 150 gulden a year. This amount would today be equal to about fifty dollars; but its purchasing power in Beethoven's day was much more. Although this was not a very great sum, it brought immediate relief to Beethoven's father and mother. Conditions were not good at home, but now that Ludwig was a wage earner, there was a ray of hope.

In the Elector's chapel Beethoven became familiar with church music; with the orchestra he acquired a knowledge of the current symphonies and concertos; and in the theater he took part in all operatic performances. He was also involved in chamber music and in light "table" music. In fact, he was wrapped up in all the musical activities then going on in the Elector's palace. There could have been no better place for musical apprenticeship.

Sitting before the keyboard of the piano or organ, Beethoven would let his fingers wander. He was not content with the notes before him and would invariably improvise his own introductions. These harmonic excursions, different at each rendering, often bewildered the singers. In Holy Week, one singer, named Heller, lost his cue and blamed it on Beethoven's improvisations. The singer was so furious that he even complained to the Elector. But the Elector was fat, generous and understanding, and only "very graciously reprimanded" the talented youth.

Beethoven became familiar with church music and also with many opera scores at this early date, but his talent lay in other directions. This is an accepted fact, yet it contains, like so many things about Beethoven, a contradiction. Although he lacked the dramatic feeling for opera, he did manage some years later, with great difficulty, to compose one opera: *Fidelio*. The overture to this opera, known as the *Leonora* overture, is most famous. Its deathless music is played by almost every symphony orchestra in the world. And although it is true that Beethoven avoided church music, still, toward the end of his musical career, when he was at the height of his creative powers, he wrote his famous *Missa Solemnis*. Of this composition Vincent d'Indy says: "We stand in the presence of one of the greatest masterworks in the realm of music."

There are these contradictions, as there are always contradictions with creative artists. But in the main, Beethoven's genius was concentrated on the symphonies. And even to his piano works he gave the scope and tonality of the orchestra. The core of his style remains instrumental.

Living in the enlightened atmosphere of the Elector's palace at a time when great social changes were in the air must certainly have had a lasting effect on his development. Thayer, his greatest biographer, says that these early social influences gave "breadth and grandeur" to his character. And these traits remained with him "through all his life."

When Beethoven was sixteen he paid a visit to Vienna, the musical capital of Europe. How this trip was managed and how he obtained the necessary funds remain to this day a mystery. It is very probable that the genial Elector encouraged the trip and paid for it. And certainly this venture was also prompted by his teacher Neefe who, some time before, had written a glowing account of young Beethoven for a magazine, which concluded with the words, "This youthful genius is deserving of help to enable him to travel."

On the authority of Anton Schindler, who was later to become Beethoven's devoted friend and his "unpaid private secretary," Beethoven is reported to have said that on this first visit to Vienna he was deeply impressed by only two persons: the Emperor Joseph II and Mozart.

Emperor Joseph II was the eldest son of Empress Maria Theresa and the brother of the Elector. If Beethoven met the Emperor, then certainly the way must have been paved by his brother, the Elector. And if the Emperor impressed the sixteen-year-old youth, it was no doubt because of a genuine admiration for his liberal views. This prince, a true son of eighteenth-century enlightenment, undertook extensive religious and civil reforms. He allowed non-Catholics freedom of worship and brought the education of the clergy under state control. He reformed the law courts, simplified taxation, restored to the people the freedom of the press, and completed the abolition of serfdom. Under his rule marriage became a civil contract. His regime was by far the most liberal prevailing in Europe at this date. And yet when this is said, it should also be said that this was the Emperor who rejected Mozart's application for court *Kapellmeister*.

There was reason enough for young Beethoven to admire this prince of enlightenment. But there is no recorded account of how the meeting took place or whether Beethoven ever played for the Emperor.

The Mozart meeting is a little more definite, but this is also shrouded in mystery. Mozart's biographer, Otto Jahn, gives an account of their meeting. "Beethoven, who was a very promising young man came to Vienna in the spring of 1787. He was taken to see Mozart who asked him to play for him which he did. Mozart, believing that he was listening to a well prepared composition, praised it rather coolly. Beethoven, aware of this, asked Mozart to give him a theme for improvisation. He always played his best when put to a test and now inspired by the presence of the Master whom he greatly respected, Beethoven began to play. Mozart's attention and interest grew more and more; at length he went quietly to some friends sitting in the adjoining room and said emphatically, 'Keep your eyes on this fellow; some day he will give the world something to talk about.' "

The true object of Beethoven's visit to Vienna has never been made clear. Did he hope at sixteen, although he believed he was only fourteen, to secure a position with some orchestra? Or did he hope to gain the friendship of Mozart and receive instruction in piano and composition? Or was there some other hidden motive? Even the lively account of Mozart's biographer, Otto Jahn, so often repeated, must be questioned. The story is one Jahn heard many years after the event is supposed to have taken place.

There is no evidence whatsoever to prove that Mozart ever warmed up to the young Beethoven. Some years later, in 1792, when Beethoven returned to make Vienna his permanent home, Mozart was dead. He had died the year before.

But Beethoven's first visit to Vienna came to an abrupt end. Here the records all agree. He had been in Vienna only about two months when he received letters from his father urging him to return with all possible speed. His mother was critically ill.

Beethoven started out by coach but got only halfway when his money ran out. To continue his journey he was forced to borrow from a friend whom he had only recently met.

He arrived home to find everything in a bad way. His mother was close to death. Beside her in a cradle lay an infant girl, also sick. The father had pawned whatever household goods he could to raise additional money. The rooms were dirty. His two younger brothers walked about aimlessly and the father was in a stupor.

Soon Beethoven's mother was dead. And a few months later the infant girl was also in her grave. This child was the fourth born to Beethoven's mother to die in infancy.

To the friend who had been kind enough to lend Beethoven the money to continue his journey he wrote a long letter, in which he described his feelings: "The nearer I came to my native city, the more letters reached me from my father urging me to hurry as my mother was not in good health. Although far from well myself I hurried on with all possible speed. The desire to be able to see my dying mother overcame every obstacle. I found her still alive but in a deplorable state; she was ill with tuberculosis, and about seven weeks ago, after suffering much pain she died. She was a kind and lovable mother to me, and my best friend. . . . I hope to obtain your forgiveness for my long silence. As for the extreme kindness you showed me in Augsburg in lending me three Carolins, I must beg you to please be indulgent with me a little longer. My journey has been a great expense and there is little hope of earning extra money in this place. Fate is not kind to me, here in Bonn." Here is the first appearance of the word "Fate." This concept, as we will see, became very important to Beethoven and greatly influenced his life and his music.

His poverty was extreme. History records that the cemetery plot in which Beethoven's mother was buried was not fully paid for. And in time another body, that of an Italian priest, was interred in the same grave. After a full century, and after much digging, her bones were finally located. She now has a grave of her own marked with a simple headstone on which are carved the words, "She was a kind and lovable mother to me, and my best friend."

Beethoven's father felt that drink might wash away his sorrows and so he drank very heavily. He was of little use to the Elector. And he was no good at home. In fact, he was of no use to anyone. The genial Elector must have known this, for six years later, when he was informed of the death of Johann Beethoven, he remarked dryly: "The liquor excise taxes have suffered a loss."

During these six years the responsibility of holding the family together rested on Beethoven. He found a cheap apartment for his drunken father and two brothers, and he hired a housekeeper to cook and look after them. He was seventeen and his brothers were then thirteen and eleven.

Before Ludwig was nineteen he was forced to petition the Elector for part of his father's salary so that he could meet the expenses of the home. This the Elector granted without delay. He dispensed with the services of the drunken father and ordered half the salary "be paid to the son, besides the salary which he now draws and the three measures of grain for the support of his brothers."

In this manner did young Beethoven become legal head of the family. He encouraged his brother Karl to take music lessons so that he might be able to join the court orchestra. His youngest brother, Johann, he apprenticed to the court apothecary. In time he might become a druggist.

Here at this early date we recognize a trait in Beethoven that was later to become characteristic of the man and his

music. He had within him the power to surmount sorrow
and misery. With a conquering will he could march on and
never bow down to adversity. The sordidness and cruel
poverty of these days left a telling mark, but he learned how
to manage with this kind of agony. He learned the lesson
of life and hope.

The five years following his mother's death which Beethoven spent in Bonn were years of work, development, recognition and, surprisingly, some happy and stimulating social
contacts. Underneath his morose, dreamy, introverted manner he had a need and a talent for making friends. Some of
the friends he made at this difficult period of his life were to
remain devoted to him to his last days. They were more than
devoted; they were understanding and helped bring forward
the best in his nature. These social contacts, which fortu-
nately came during his formative years—the years between
seventeen and twenty-two—helped him to emerge from the
dark pit of his family environment.

It was the von Breuning family that had the greatest influence on Beethoven. Madame von Breuning was a charming and cultured widow with four happy children, three boys
and a girl. The eldest boy was a year younger than Beethoven; the youngest boy was only ten; and the attractive girl,
Eleonora, was fifteen. Beethoven gave the children piano
lessons and Madame von Breuning, recognizing his unusual
qualities, befriended him. She felt that he needed a mother
and she treated him as one of her own family. His neglected
nature, warmed by affection, slowly unfolded and blossomed.

In this happy atmosphere his blunt manners became less
awkward, his clothes less slovenly, and his shyness dimin-
ished. When Beethoven fell into one of his morbid brooding

moods, Madame von Breuning would say, "He is in a rapture." In later life he often repeated these words to describe his inturned moody nature. All his life he remembered this noble woman and spoke of her as his "guardian angel." To her son Stephan he later dedicated his famous violin concerto and to her daughter Eleonora a sonata and a set of variations.

It was in the home of the von Breunings that Beethoven met a young medical student whose name was Franz Gerhard Wegeler. He was destined to be one of Beethoven's closest friends. Wegeler became a professor of medicine and married Eleonora von Breuning.

The von Breuning family was nourished on music and literature. It was here that Beethoven heard Homer and Plutarch read in Greek, which he was able to follow with the aid of a translation. All his life he remembered the great dignity and heroic splendor of blind Homer. Here was a defiance of Fate and a courage that knew no defeat. Here were heroic conceptions which were forceful and capable of inspiring a new music.

Beethoven's days in the Elector's palace had taken on a happier aspect. He was now chief organist and chief pianist. He also played the viola in the orchestra which, due to the efforts of the Elector, had grown until it rivaled the best in Europe. Beethoven was popular with his fellow musicians, who now looked upon him, not as a promising youth, but as a great pianist.

A chaplain named Junker heard Beethoven play in the Elector's palace and described it as most unusual. He greatly admired Beethoven's "almost inexhaustible wealth of ideas, the altogether characteristic style of expression, and the great execution he displays. . . . Yet he is exceedingly modest and

and free from all pretensions. . . . His style of treating his
instrument is as different from that usually adopted, that it
impresses one with the idea that by a path of his own dis-
covery he has attained that height of excellence whereon he
now stands."

There was another admirer of Beethoven's playing who
proved a great deal more important to his musical career
than Junker. This was the aristocrat, Count Ferdinand Ernst
Gabriel Waldstein, an Austrian nobleman. He had come to
Bonn to be made a Knight of the Teutonic Order. His good
friend the Elector was the Grand Master of the Order.

Waldstein, who was eight years older than Beethoven, was
himself an amateur musician. During his days in Bonn, while
he was going through the training and ritual required of
every Knight of the Teutonic Order, he struck up a happy
friendship with the young virtuoso. He went to Beethoven's
room almost daily. They made music together but more often
Beethoven improvised on the piano. He felt at ease with
Waldstein, and Waldstein—quick to recognize the unusual
talent of Beethoven—cast about for ways to help him.

The first thing he did was to send Beethoven a new piano.
Then he managed to get him a little extra money, pretending
that it came from the Elector. He also gave Beethoven a commission to compose a ballet for him which he could pass off
as his own. This was a common custom of the day; in fact,
Mozart's last composition, his famous *Requiem,* was written
for a patron who intended to have it performed as his own
composition. Beethoven was a most willing "ghost" and wrote
the music for the *Ritterballet* which was later performed as a
composition by Count Waldstein.

Beethoven received a great deal from his friends, in this

period of his life. In return he only played for them. But time has fully sponged out any indebtedness. The von Breunings would be forgotten today except for the kindness they showed Beethoven. And as for the good Austrian count who came to Bonn to become Knight of the Teutonic Order, little did he suspect that the composition dedicated to him and known to the world as the *Waldstein Sonata* would become immortal. His name, now attached to this music, lives on.

Count Waldstein encouraged Beethoven in many ways. It is believed by many biographers that Waldstein was the first to urge Beethoven to leave Bonn and go to Vienna to study composition under Haydn. Waldstein may well have suggested this to his friend the Elector and prevailed upon him to give Beethoven leave of absence on full salary.

This may have been the case but the Elector was also thinking of departing from Bonn, for in neighboring France that social convulsion known as revolution was in full swing. The Bastille had fallen three years before. From that moment on the crowns of Europe were uneasy. The year before, 1791, the King of France and his Queen Marie Antoinette attempted to escape into Belgium. But their carriage was turned back and they became the prisoners of the people of France. The French armies were on the march. And in the spring of 1792 the Elector's native Austria declared war on France. By October French troops were already marching on the Rhine and refugees began pouring into Bonn. A citizens' militia was quickly formed and the Elector's treasury removed to Düsseldorf for safety.

With these troubles plaguing him, the Elector had no time for music. But at any rate he did give consent to Beethoven's departure at full pay, and this may have been done at Waldstein's suggestion. What good was an extra organist in a palace that would soon be empty?

Beethoven packed as fast as he could. His coach for Vienna left at six o'clock, in the dark of the morning of November 2 or 3. The Elector had already fled from Bonn two or three days before.

Beethoven had spent his first twenty-two years in Bonn. He knew the beautiful fields, vineyards and hills which were laced together by the winding river Rhine. Here were the memories of his youth. And out of these memories grew his deep love for nature, a love that remained with him to his last day.

Many years later he said to his old and devoted friend Wegeler, "My fatherland, the beautiful region in which I first saw the light, is still clear and beautiful before my eyes."

But all this he was now leaving behind and a new world, the musical world of Vienna, was to open before him. And Bonn, the town of his birth, and his beautiful Rhineland, he was never to see again.

3

VIENNA

O N HIS way to Vienna an event took place which fired his imagination and no doubt left a deep impression on his mind. War was in the air. Everyone knew that the French armies were on the march and that other armies were going out to meet these invaders. But Beethoven little expected to see any signs of trouble.

Before reaching Coblenz his coach ran into the advancing Hessian army. Beethoven recorded in his notebook that he gave the coachman a tip "because the fellow drove like the devil through the Hessian army at the risk of a cudgeling."

This was his first brush with a military machine. Later he was to reflect on war, defeat and victory in his famous *Eroica* symphony and also in a very inferior rattletrap composition entitled *Wellington's Victory, or the Battle of Vittoria.* Coming at the time of Napoleon's defeat this inferior composition was a great popular success. It brought Beethoven fame in England and in other parts of Europe. He even conducted this descriptive piece of music for the sovereigns of Europe when they gathered in the Congress of Vienna in 1815. But this was later. His first brush with soldiers was on the way to Vienna.

Beethoven arrived in Vienna in 1792. Five years before he had been here on the brief visit which had been cut short by the illness of his mother. But now he had come to stay. From now on Vienna was to become his home. This was the musical capital of Europe. Here he felt he belonged.

The city was the same as it had been five years before, except that Mozart had died a year ago. The good prince of the Enlightenment, Joseph II, was also dead and on the Austrian throne sat his brother, Leopold II.

The Vienna of this period has been described as a place of indolence, ignorance and fears. It had a population of almost 400,000.

The general public was little influenced by the spirit of enlightenment and justice which had come to Austria through Joseph II. The war with Napoleon had brought in reaction and had wiped out the free press and other liberal gains. For centuries the people had been bowed down by servility. They were still under the drumbeat of discipline. The belief that the king's rule was the divine will of God had been instilled over the centuries. The government had always been brutal, although now it was a little less brutal. Dread and fear gripped the general public. The revolution in France, which imprisoned the Austrian Marie Antoinette, brought back the iron hand which crushed all liberal ideas.

In the coffeehouses rumors were circulated, rumors of palace happenings, backstairs gossip, rumors of wars, new laws for conscripts, and rumors about the Austrian army which was then somewhere in Europe, though no one knew exactly where. Nothing was frankly out in the open. There was a love of indirectness, of intrigue, of whispering. Every family had one or more men in the army. Everything was held secret. Letters often were forbidden. Men were killed or missing and never again heard from. This was part of the life of the times.

In the fifteen previous years Austria had lost over a million men in wars created only out of a monarch's greed. Royal marriages with France and Italy, as well as other alliances, had failed to bolster a declining empire. For five centuries the Hapsburgs had ruled by war, blood and iron.

The people of Vienna were used to wars. The cloak of suspicion and fear that hung over them was an old cloak. There were secret police all over Vienna. At one time they numbered 10,000. Servants in homes listened and reported. Everyone was watched. Everyone was spied upon. The ugly and brutal Hapsburgs crushed all individuality. And yet the people were gay! They were accustomed to unrest, to wars, to police surveillance. They knew little of the world outside. Their newspapers were censored. Vienna was an island. Yet the people made it a happy island.

Books were suppressed, circulating libraries forbidden, plays and operas were censored. But no objection was found to music. And because of this music was free. And other things, also, were very free. Wine flowed freely. Good food was enjoyed. Vienna had a merry night life, licentious and disorderly. The people wanted desperately to be happy, and so nothing was taken too seriously.

Mozart had noticed this when he came to Vienna. He summed up the character of the people in a letter to a friend: "The Viennese—so to speak generally—are not eager for anything serious and sensible and have little or no understanding of it. They care for nothing but utter trash, burlesques, harlequinades, ghost tricks, farces and devil's antics. Their theaters furnish proof of this daily. You may see a fine gentleman, even with an order on his breast, laughing until tears run down his face and applauding with all his might some senseless buffoonery or simple joke." With keen intuition Mozart put his finger on the chief trouble. He blamed it all on the character of the court and on the Emperor.

But to all this one must add an important trait. The people of Vienna were friendly, affectionate, generous and warmhearted.

It was to this Vienna that Beethoven came in the month of November, 1792.

This time Beethoven was no longer a shy poor boy with a ruddy pockmarked face, ashamed of his blunt Rhenish accent. Yes, the pockmarks and his protruding front teeth and his accent were still there, but he now walked with an air of assurance. He was master of the keyboard and he knew that he could play his way into favor.

Inside he felt confident. And perhaps, too, his years of happy contact with the cultured von Breuning family had made him a little more social, had polished off some of his crudeness. For now he was dressed in a fine tailor-made coat, a powdered wig and silk stockings. He was armed with letters of introduction, probably given him by the Elector and Count Waldstein.

No time at all was lost. He merely rang the bell and the doors of the mansions were opened and flunkies ushered him in.

When he first arrived he rented a room in an attic. But he

soon moved to the ground floor and in a little over a year he was living in the palatial home of Prince Karl Lichnowsky. This prince, who was about twelve years older than Beethoven, had once been a pupil of Mozart. He had a genuine love of music. He was quick to recognize Beethoven's genius and invited him to live as a guest in his home. To this he added 600 gulden a year, which Beethoven might draw upon until the time came when he did not require such funds. And to spare the feelings of his protégé, the prince ordered the palace servants to answer his bell first.

All this and more. A horse and groom were set aside for Beethoven, although there is no record of anyone ever having seen him riding in the park. But more important than the horse was the Prince's private orchestra and his fine string quartet. These were placed at Beethoven's disposal. Some years later this private orchestra had the honor of playing the first performance of Beethoven's now famous *Eroica* symphony. All this and still more! Prince Lichnowsky himself practiced Beethoven's piano works and played them to prove to all Vienna that the music was not too difficult and that its dramatic effects could be produced even by amateurs like himself.

Many of the Viennese nobility were fine musicians. The Princess Lichnowsky was a good pianist; so also was the Baroness von Ertmann. Prince Lobkowitz was an able violinist and Count Esterhazy played both the viola and oboe and Count Brunswick managed fairly well on the cello. The Russian ambassador to Austria, Count Razoumowsky, who was related by marriage to Prince Lichnowsky, was a good musician and often played in quartets. His name is famous today, not because of his diplomatic services to the Czar, but only

because of his friendship with Beethoven. It was he who commissioned the most loved of all Beethoven's quartets: that famous set of three, now known as the *Razoumowsky Quartets*.

It was in the home of Prince Lichnowsky that Beethoven
met most of the aristocratic musical amateurs in Vienna, as
well as many others who fell under the compelling spell of his
music and remained devoted friends. They brought him presents and they cut quill pens for him, for his fingers were very
clumsy except when on the keyboard. It was here, too, that
he met Hummel the pianist and other famous musicians,
many of whom were friends of Haydn and had known
Mozart.

But luxury seemed to get in Beethoven's way. He could not
surrender to the life in the Prince's palace and he complained
to friends that the four o'clock meal in the afternoon was
often inconvenient, for he had to stop his work to shave and
wash and dress—all for what? And so, after the novelty of
living in a palace had worn off, he moved to rooms of his
own.

Soon some of his old Bonn intimates joined him in Vienna.
There was Wegeler, the former medical student who had
married Beethoven's pupil, Eleonora von Breuning. Her two
brothers, Stephen and Lorenz, had also come to Vienna, as
well as Reiche, the flute player from the Bonn orchestra.

Few men ever had so rich a battalion of friends in so short
a time after arriving in a new city.

About a month after Beethoven reached Vienna he learned
of the death of his father. His death was unmourned. Later
it was discovered that his passion for liquor had driven him

to embezzlement. He had taken the money which Beethoven had left behind for the support of his younger brothers.

As for the Elector, who had fled from Bonn two days before Beethoven left, he had hoped to come back to his little kingdom. But the success of the French Revolutionary armies prevented his return. Since he could not levy taxes on his peasants, his treasury reduced the salary payments promised Beethoven and in six months stopped them altogether. The Elector became a wandering ruler without his little monarchy. Five years later the electorate became part of the Republic of France.

Beethoven's two younger brothers, Karl and Johann, soon followed him to Vienna. But now they were no longer a burden on him. Johann was a full-fledged apothecary. And Karl, who had, with little talent, tried hard to be a musician, became a cashier in a bank.

These first few years in Vienna were happy years for Beethoven. This is the only period in his life when we find him free from troubles. The bitterness of his early childhood had now sweetened. Fortune had smiled.

He lived in a genial and friendly society. He went from one great home to another giving lessons, making music, displaying himself and basking in the glow of admiration. He dressed in fashion. He even took dancing lessons, but he soon gave them up because he could never bring rhythm down into his feet.

From time to time he contested with renowned pianists in the homes of the aristocracy. This was a favorite pastime. Mozart and the brilliant Italian pianist Clementi had once engaged in such a keyboard contest before royalty. Often the

pianists were asked to improvise on a theme which was given
them.

In these contests, Beethoven, who was a master at improvisation, always emerged the victor. And these public exhibi-
tions helped greatly to give him an outstanding reputation.
One virtuoso, the Bohemian Gelinek, admitting his defeat,
said, "Beethoven is no man; he's a devil. He will play me and
all of us to death. And how he improvises!"

The renowned pianist whom Beethoven managed to out-
shine in public considered him a deadly rival. And he, too,
in these early days, considered them as enemies. He even de-
vised schemes that would show up their keyboard defects.
Writing to Eleonora von Breuning, after he had been in
Vienna only about a year, he said, "I take the liberty of sending you these Variations and Rondo for Piano and Violin. . . .
The Variations will be somewhat difficult to play, especially
the trills in the coda; but do not let this discourage you." He
then explained that he wrote them in this way because people
tried to imitate his playing and, also, "There is another reason:
to embarrass the Viennese piano virtuosi. Many of them are
my mortal enemies and so I wish to take my revenge in this
way. I know these variations will be submitted to them and
they are bound to give a poor account of themselves."

But before long the Viennese piano virtuosi ceased to be
his "mortal enemies." With his wonderful rendering of Bach's
Well-tempered Clavier, and with the robust originality and
the highly imaginative quality of his improvisations, he was
soon recognized as the outstanding master. Never again did
he feel the urge to write music merely to display the defects
of inferior pianists.

It was during these happy early days in Vienna that Beethoven took lessons from the famous Haydn. But somehow or other, the lessons, which continued for over a year, proved a disappointing failure. Beethoven had expected more from Haydn and Haydn was not impressed with Beethoven. They opposed each other temperamentally. Beethoven felt that Haydn was careless in correcting his exercises in harmony. And when he showed him his three trios, Op. 1, Haydn praised the one which Beethoven felt was the worst, and because of this he questioned Haydn's sincerity. As for Haydn, he certainly could not have liked Beethoven's arrogance, nor could he have been pleased with his musical innovations and other harmonic liberties.

At the end of a year both were happy when the lessons ended. Later Beethoven said, "Though I had some instruction from Haydn, I never learned anything from him." This is a strong statement and one that has been challenged by modern biographers and musicologists. Vincent d'Indy in his study of Beethoven says, "Papa Haydn taught him to discriminate, to dispose his musical elements in logical fashion —in a word, to construct, which is the whole art of the composer, and so Beethoven . . . remained profoundly grateful to his master; a thousand details might be cited to prove it." Haydn's last period certainly influenced Beethoven's early compositions.

His keyboard knowledge came from Karl Philipp Emanuel Bach, but from Haydn he gathered his architectural sense of composition.

Yet, in spite of all their hearty disregard for each other, they remained friends. Eventually they became even better friends. In time Haydn was more forthcoming with his praise. And at the first performance of Haydn's *Creation*, Beethoven, deeply moved, came to the wheelchair and kissed the old man's hand and forehead. Haydn had lived to understand the young composer's harmonic innovations, and Beethoven, now famous, could well afford to be humble and generous.

Determined to learn more of harmony and counterpoint, Beethoven took lessons from Albrechtsberger, and also from Mozart's rival, Salieri, who had formerly been the conductor of the opera and court *Kapellmeister*. Salieri taught him vocal composition, verbal accent, meter and rhythm.

"I knew them all well," wrote Ferdinand Ries of the three teachers. The young Ries, son of the violinist in the Bonn orchestra, had come to Vienna to study piano with Beethoven. All three teachers valued Beethoven highly, but all were of one mind regarding his habits of study. They all said Beethoven was too headstrong and too self-reliant. "He just refused to accept things presented in lessons. He had to learn everything through hard experience."

Compared to Mozart, who at the age of twenty-two had already written forty symphonies and three hundred other compositions, Beethoven was slow in developing as a composer, but the little he had written bore his very individual stamp. Although his epoch-making *Eroica* symphony and the *Waldstein* and *Appassionata* sonatas were still twelve years away, in the opinion of Burk, one of the keenest modern Beethoven authorities, "Beethoven did not go to Haydn to learn how to compose. He was then already a composer, a skilled and finished one." Burk is also of the opinion that "the imagination of Beethoven was to enliven, and turn into the forms of beauty," even the dry and uninspired exercises that his teachers gave him.

But the fact remains that he developed slowly and almost

painfully. His few compositions were still without opus number. Some of these he later revised and numbered.

At this time Beethoven considered himself a pianist and not a composer. His art was the art of the keyboard. And as a virtuoso he won friends and admiration. "What more do I expect?" he asked. He developed this talent and superior keyboard technique with the full assurance that it would not only attract attention but also bring him money.

Only a few years later did the great tragedy of his life announce itself. When he began losing his hearing, he knew that his days as a concert performer were not long. Then, with a heart weighted with sorrow, he turned to composition.

Had Beethoven died before he was thirty his name would have been a footnote on a page of musical history. He would have been remembered only as a keyboard virtuoso.

But to hear him play must have been a memorable experience. From all accounts his playing was different from anything known at the time. His whole approach to the keyboard was different.

Karl Czerny, who came to Beethoven as a young boy, describes their first meeting. "I played Mozart's great *C Major Concerto*, which begins with a series of chords. Beethoven was at once attentive; he came closer to my chair and in those passages where the piano merely accompanies the orchestra he played the orchestra melody with his left hand. His hands were densely covered with hair and his fingers, especially at the tips, were very broad. . . . During the first lessons Beethoven occupied me exclusively with scales in all the keys, showed me the only right position of the hands, still unknown to most players at that time, the position of

the fingers and especially the use of the thumb. The useful-
ness of these principles I did not fully appreciate until a
much later time. After this he made me play the exercises in
Emanuel Bach's textbook. And he drew my attention to the
legato, which he had himself mastered in a marvelous manner and which at the time other pianists considered unnecessary, for it was then still the fashion, dating from Mozart's
time, to play in a clipped, abrupt manner."

By this we see that Beethoven departed from the fashion
of the day. The Mozart style of piano playing did not suit his
nature. He could imitate the clean-cut cameo style with all
its elegance and tonal discourses played with a bony per-
cussion technique. But this was not his idea of how the music
and the piano should sound. He loved a broad, big, grand
style, orchestral in manner, one that allowed for color,
bright outlines and deep shadows. He liked his notes to be
sustained like organ tones and his phrasing unbroken and
smooth as the drawing of a violin bow.

Some critics thought him guilty of sustaining the sound
through a heavy use of the pedal. Lacking lacy elegance, he
was charged with being a rough player.

But Czerny says that no one equaled him in the rapidity
of his scales, double trills and skips. To gain his effects he
used both pedals far more frequently than indicated in the
written music. "His bearing while playing was masterfully
quiet, noble and beautiful; without the slightest grimace, he
only bent forward as his deafness grew upon him. His fingers
were very powerful, not long, and broadened at the tips."

About Beethoven's wonderful talent for improvisation
Czerny has recorded that it "was most brilliant and amazing.

In whatever kind of society he might find himself he was able to make so deep an impression on his listeners that often not a single eye remained dry, and there were some who broke out in loud sobs. Besides the beauty and the originality of his ideas and his spirited manner of expressing them, there was something magical about his playing." Seeing the tears of his listeners when he had ended playing, he would laugh and say, as though he were vexed, "You are a crowd of fools." Sometimes, pretending to be offended, he asked, "Who can live among such spoilt children?"

Here in Karl Czerny's account we have the first recognition of that magical secret power in Beethoven's music. This emotional power is first discovered in his improvisations. And this same power we now know through his compositions.

In this lie the heart and soul of Beethoven. As Ernest Newman, the English music critic, says, "It is a peculiarity of Beethoven's imagination, that time and time again he lifts us to a height from which we evaluate not only all music but all life, all emotion and all thought."

The power to transfer this imagination, through the keyboard, to his listeners and to bring tears to their eyes was already evident in those early hopeful and happy days in Vienna. This came before the tragedy of his deafness. Beethoven was then not the Beethoven that is stamped so vividly on our minds: a Beethoven subject to ungovernable fits of bad temper, suspicious, unpleasant in manner, rude without reason, arrogant and totally devoid of consideration or politeness. All this came later.

It is important to note that he possessed his magical power of imagination in the early Vienna days and before deafness

closed the world of sound to him. The magic did not stem
from his deafness. His loss of hearing only intensified the
tragic sense of life and passionate struggle that was already
rooted deep in his creative nature.

4

LOVE OF
THE THREE COUNTESSES

THREE young countesses suddenly entered Beethoven's life, bringing him romance and love. The year was 1799, seven years after he had arrived in Vienna.

Countess Therese von Brunswick records how she and her sister Countess Josephine, accompanied by their mother, climbed the three flights of stairs to visit Beethoven. Therese was twenty-four and her sister Josephine was twenty.

"I entered with my Beethoven trio for piano, violin and cello under my arm, like a little girl going to her lesson. The dear immortal Beethoven was most amiable, and as polite as he could be. After a few introductory remarks he placed me at his out-of-tune piano, and I began at once. I played bravely and sang the violin and cello accompaniment. He was so delighted that he promised to come each day to our hotel. . . . He kept his word. But instead of staying for an hour after midday he would stay four or five."

In this way did romance begin. The third attractive

countess to come into Beethoven's life was a cousin of the von Brunswicks, the sixteen-year-old Countess Giulietta Guicciardi. She arrived the following year, 1800. Beethoven loved all three. He was always in love.

The von Brunswicks were an old noble Hungarian family who traced their ancestry back to the crusaders. Count von Brunswick, the father of the children, was a gentleman of culture. He adored music and was impressed with the American Revolution. "I was brought up," says his eldest daughter Therese, "with the names Washington and Benjamin Franklin." This republican spirit no doubt helped make the family attractive to Beethoven.

On their vast estate in Hungary Therese began playing the piano when she was three years old. There were four children in the family, three girls and a boy. Some years after the father died, the mother, who was a very masterful and domineering woman, packed up her four children and brought them to Vienna. Besides the two eldest girls, Therese and Josephine, there was Charlotte, who was then seventeen, and their attractive twenty-two-year-old brother, Franz.

Beethoven was pleased to give lessons to the two eldest girls. It pleased him to hear his sonatas played by these pretty and cultured young aristocrats. As for Franz, he was an accomplished cello player and in time he became one of Beethoven's cherished friends. A dozen years after their first meeting we find Beethoven writing to Franz and addressing him, "Dear friend and brother." And it was to this devoted Franz von Brunswick that the wonderful *Appassionata Sonata* was dedicated.

Once more, as it had been in Bonn with the charming and cultured von Breuning household, Beethoven was brought into intimate family life. The von Brunswicks did everything to put him at ease and make him feel important and welcome. And when their time in Vienna was up and they had to return to Hungary, they induced Beethoven to follow them.

"It was then," records the Countess Therese, "that there sprang up between Beethoven and us the intimate friendship, the friendship of the heart, that endured to the end of his days." Beethoven often visited this country home and was received by what Therese called "our social republic of distinguished people." In the private park of this estate lime trees had been planted within a circular space. And each tree had been given the name of one of their friends. One tree was named Beethoven. The young romantic Countess Therese recorded that she was able to communicate with these trees by secret signs and that the trees would reply to her questions. Often in the morning she would go to this grove and talk to the trees and the trees would tell her everything she desired to know. "Never did a tree refuse to reply."

It was this kind of imagination and love of nature that brought Therese and Beethoven close together. She had in her the kind of nobility he felt in his heart. She gave him an inner courage. It is very possible that the penciled note written on a page of his notebook at this time was inspired by Therese. "You are now plunged into the social whirlpool and so it is possible to compose operas in spite of your social obstacles. Let your deafness no longer be a secret, even in art."

But it was Josephine, who was four years younger than Therese and by far the more attractive, who really captured Beethoven's heart. Although both sisters were attracted to Beethoven and both were affectionately attached to him, it is believed, from the flimsy evidence at hand, that Josephine held first place in his heart.

However, about a year after they met Beethoven, the mother married off the attractive young Countess Josephine to a man who was fifty years old. Josephine, who had been reaching out for an artistic life, one that had in it some spiritual meaning, found herself tied to a stupid, middle-aged count and to a life that was humdrum and tedious. In her helplessness she turned to Beethoven.

But after three years the dull-witted count died, leaving Josephine, a pretty widow, with four children and a heavy load of financial worries. It was during the summer after the death of the Count that Beethoven came out to the country and rented a place not far from Josephine.

Therese felt that she had been supplanted in Beethoven's affections by her sister. From time to time she received news of this romance from her youngest sister Charlotte. "Beethoven is extraordinarily amiable. He comes every day and stays with Josephine for hours." A month later she expresses her fears in a letter to Therese and wonders what is going to happen to her sister and Beethoven. "She must look out!"

In the same year, 1800, that the pretty Josephine was married to the dull, middle-aged count, the third young and pretty countess—Giulietta Guicciardi—came into Beethoven's life. Beethoven fell madly in love with this sixteen-year-old Italian Juliet. The von Brunswick countesses considered her a serious rival. They spoke of her winning high favor in the Vienna salons and called her *"la belle Guicciardi."*

Beethoven had even hoped that marriage might open for him the path to happiness. In a letter to his intimate friend

Wegeler, Beethoven wrote: "Now my life is a little more agreeable again, for I mix more in society. . . . This change has been brought about by a charming, fascinating girl who loves me and whom I love. . . . And this is the first time I have ever felt that marriage could make one happy. Unfortunately she is not of my social standing, and besides I could not marry at present; I must still struggle on."

He gave Giulietta lessons for about three years. Then suddenly he learned of her marriage to a certain Count Gallenberg. This was a great shock. The news came to him when he was living in the country and when his spirits were at a very low ebb. With his romantic hope dashed and with his oncoming deafness, Beethoven fell into a state of depression which produced an important crisis in his life.

Many years after this passionate romance had cooled, Beethoven confessed to Schindler, "I was well loved by her, and more than her husband ever loved her."

After Beethoven died, a little miniature of Giulietta and one of Therese were found in a secret drawer in his desk, together with that mysterious document known as the letter written to the "Immortal Beloved." Who was Beethoven's "Immortal Beloved"? And why was the letter never sent? Was the "Immortal Beloved" one of the three young countesses who came into Beethoven's life just before he entered that wonderful "second period" of his creative work?

Or was the "Immortal Beloved" some other woman? We know from his pupil Ries that he had charmed many women. "He was frequently in love, but generally only for a short period. Once when I teased him about his conquest of a pretty woman he admitted that she held him in the strongest bonds for the longest time, namely, a full seven months."

5

THE ENIGMA OF
THE IMMORTAL BELOVED

H ERE is the document of the "Immortal Beloved." It is important to us today not because it is shrouded in mystery, but because it shows the heart of genius at white heat.

On the 6th of July, in the morning. My angel, my all, my very self—only a few words today and written with your pencil. . . . Why this deep sadness when necessity speaks? How can our love continue except through sacrifices, though not longing for the utmost? Can you help it that you are not wholly mine, and that I am not wholly yours? Oh, God! Look into the loveliness of nature and comfort your heart with a sense of the inevitable—love demands everything and rightfully so, thus it is for me with you and for you with me. Only you are apt to forget that I must live for myself and for you as well. Were we wholly united you would feel the pain of it as little as I. . . . I cannot tell you now all my thoughts during the past few days about my life. If only our hearts were united once and for

all I should not have such thoughts. My heart is full and
ready to tell many things. Ah! There are moments in which
I feel that speech is powerless. Be of good cheer and remain
my true, my only treasure, my all, as I am yours. The gods
must send us the rest, that which must be for us and ought
to be.

Your faithful Ludwig

Evening. Monday. July 6.

You are suffering, my dearest love. I have just found out that
letters leave here only on Mondays and Thursdays. The mail
goes from here to K. You are suffering. Ah, wherever I am,
there you are with me. I will arrange for us both. I will arrange things so that I can live with you, what a life ! ! ! But
without you ! ! However much you love me, my love for you
is the stronger. But never hide your thoughts from me. Good
night. . . . Oh God, so near! So far! Is not our love a truly
celestial mansion and as solid as heaven's vault?

Good Morning on July 7.

Even from my bed my thoughts go out to you, my Immortal
Beloved. At moments my thoughts are joyful and at times
sad while waiting to hear whether fate will take pity on us.
Either I must live wholly with you or not at all. Yes, I have
resolved to wander far from you until I can fly to your arms
and feel that I am really at home. . . . Be brave because you
know I am faithful to you and never can another possess my
heart, never never. . . . Your love makes me the happiest and
at the same time unhappiest of mortals. At my age I now need
a quiet, regular life. Is this possible in our situation? My
Angel, I have just learned that the post goes every day and I
must close so you can receive the letter without delay. Be
calm, only by calm consideration of our existence can we
attain our aim to live together. Be calm—love me—today—
yesterday—what longings I have for you—you—my life—my

all—farewell. Oh, keep on loving me—never misjudge the
faithful heart of your beloved. L.
ever yours
ever mine
ever for one another

Passion has spoken. The heart has been opened.

There has been much speculation and research. Marion M.
Scott in *Beethoven* says, "Schindler thought it had been
written in 1801 to Giulietta Guicciardi; Thayer favors 1806
or 1807 and Therese von Brunswick. Romain Rolland now
considers the date settled as 1812 and champions Therese
von Brunswick."

Some critics feel the "Immortal Beloved" was the Countess
Josephine. Amalie Sebald and Bettina Brentano are also
named, but neither of them seems to fit fully the circum-
stance and the year 1812.

As already noted, the great significance today of the "Immortal Beloved" letter is not in its mystery. It offers a unique
and rare view into the deeply passionate and longing heart
of a genius. And it attempts to put into words, which to
Beethoven were always a weak and deficient means of communication, some of the tender and passionate ideas and
feelings, charged with quiet desperation, that he has expressed in music.

If the date of the Immortal Beloved letter is established as
1812, then this letter was written long after Beethoven
learned of the marriage of Giulietta and long after that summer in which he went through a serious crisis. It was this
crisis that produced the famous Heiligenstadt Testament and

changed the course of music. This change ushered in a new period in Beethoven's creative life.

But before we leave Vienna for the quiet countryside of Heiligenstadt and the crisis that changed the course of music there is a page that must be written about Beethoven's relations with women. These are shrouded in mystery. They remain an enigma compounded only by supposition.

Vincent d'Indy insists that Beethoven's life was ruled by three passions: love of women; love of nature; and love of country. The love of nature has already been indicated and more of this is yet to come. His love of country will be difficult to uphold for he never really objected when his homeland became part of France, nor later when it became part of Prussia. And so he was inconsistent and a little confused about his love of country.

But there was nothing inconsistent about his love for women. This was definite. There was hardly a time when he was not passionately in love. His pupil Ries tells of Beethoven's great fondness for women, "especially if they had young and pretty faces." He describes how, when they were walking in the streets of Vienna and chanced to pass a pretty woman, "he would turn back and gaze keenly at her through his glasses. And if he noticed that I was watching him, he would laugh or grin. He was often in love, but usually for a short period."

Before coming to Vienna Beethoven left behind, in Bonn, several pretty girls with whom he had had flirtations. He even wrote to one of them, the attractive Babette Koch, daughter of the innkeeper in whose tavern he often had his meals. In fact, he wrote her twice but she never bothered to reply.

The information that has come down to us about Beethoven's romances is fragmentary. On doubtful evidence much has been supposed and much has been written. The women in Beethoven's life are important only because, through affection, they sustained, nourished and warmed the inner creative forces of the artist. But much of Beethoven's creative inspiration did not come from his love of women. His physical needs and his spiritual needs were independent of each other.

And throughout his life he was secretive about the women he loved. A century of research has not been able to identify definitely Beethoven's "Immortal Beloved."

6

THE WORLD OF
SOUND GROWS DIM

B EETHOVEN's pupil Czerny, who first came to him about
1798, records that at the time "he did not show the
slightest sign of being hard of hearing." He also noted that
when Beethoven sat at the piano he leaned forward and bent
his head very low to hear the sound better. But this seemed
his accustomed position and it aroused no suspicion.

However, it was in this year, or very soon after, that Beethoven began to notice that there was something wrong with
his hearing. The doctors whom he consulted were unable to
bring him relief. For a long time he did not dare breathe a
word about it to anyone.

Only when he was able to admit to himself that the treatments seemed useless and that his condition was growing
worse did he confide to an intimate friend who lived far from
Vienna. This letter was written almost two years after the
trouble first came to his notice. It was written to Karl

[52]

Amende, who was a country vicar. "My dear, good Amende, my loyal Friend . . . How often do I wish you were with me, for your Beethoven lives most unhappily, in discord with nature and his Creator. Often have I cursed him for exposing his creatures to chance, so that often the loveliest blossoms are destroyed. I must confide to you that my hearing has sadly deteriorated. I knew this at the time we last saw each other but I was silent. Now it has grown progressively worse. Whether it can be cured remains to be seen. They say the trouble was caused by the condition of my bowels which are now fully recovered. But will my hearing also get better? I sincerely hope so but I doubt it because such conditions are most incurable. How miserably I must now live avoiding all that is dear and precious to me. . . . Must I take refuge in sad resignation! I have resolved to raise myself above all this but how will that be possible? . . . My affliction causes me the least trouble in playing and in composition but most in my association with others. . . . I beg you to treat this matter of my hearing as a great secret, which you must not betray to anyone at all."

A few weeks later he wrote to his old friend Dr. Wegeler, "My poor health is a jealous demon and is ever putting a spoke in my wheel. By this I mean that for the last three years my hearing has grown steadily worse. . . . My ears whistle and buzz continually day and night. . . . I have avoided all social gatherings for how is it possible for me to tell people, 'I am deaf'. . . . To give you an idea of this curious condition I must tell you that in the theater I must get close to the stage in order to hear the actors. If I am at a slight distance then the high notes of instruments and singers I do not hear at all. I can often hear the low tones of a conversation but I cannot make out the words. It is strange that in conversation people do not notice my lack of hearing but they seem to attribute my behavior to my absence of mind. When people speak softly I hear tones but not the words. I cannot bear to be yelled at. Heavens knows what will come of this. I have often cursed my Creator. . . . Yet I am determined to resist my fate, although I know that there will be times when I shall be God's most unhappy creature."

Beethoven was thirty-one years old when he wrote these confiding letters. His deafness grew worse year by year. Until he was forty-seven years old he did hear a little. At times he seemed to hear better than at other times. But the last ten years of his life he lived in the silent world of the totally deaf.

For years he hoped that baths, ointments or other medicines might possibly have good effect. He tried everything. At times he seemed desperate. He feared that his "enemies" might learn of his trouble. Every rival he believed to be an "enemy." He also feared that, if his hearing got worse, he would have to give up his concert work. And this was, at last, bringing him financial returns. To hide his handicap and defend the source of his income, he pretended that he was absent-minded.

Little by little his fears grew. Now and then he put on a brave front and with pride declared that he would surmount illness and distress and drive on to triumph. This ring of triumph in which life lifts itself out of defeat and marches boldly on is very noticeable in his music. His letters and his conversations, however, are filled with complaint and self-pity. He is suspicious of his servants, his friends, his publishers, his copyists and even his patrons. He complains about his illness, about the lack of appreciation and the low musical taste of the Viennese.

And so here again we are confronted with a strange contradiction. On all evidence there is little nobility in his character. Yet, again and again, the noble and the heroic is encountered in his life and it rings out clearly in his music. With his growing deafness he became more and more disagreeable. And more and more did his music soar to rare and sublime heights.

The deafness grew very slowly. It was most worrying but Beethoven was still able to perform at concerts, give lessons to his pupils, improvise before admiring gatherings and compose works for the piano as well as compositions for orchestra and chamber groups.

By 1801, when he confided the secret of his growing deafness, his main compositions included his first symphony, his first two piano concertos, three piano trios, two sonatas for piano and violoncello, three string trios, a song entitled *Adelaide* which ran through many editions, and his first fifteen piano sonatas. These sonatas included the well-known and much played *Sonata Pathétique* in which, according to Burk, Beethoven steps forth as a "poet of melancholy," and also the famous *Moonlight Sonata* in which, also on the excellent authority of Burk, we find "the first of the tumultuous outbursts of stormy passion which Beethoven was about to let loose through the piano sonatas."

This music is so familiar to us that it is difficult to believe that at that time people complained—complained because this new music did not have the customary sweetness, was overdramatic, and its dissonance grated on sensitive ears. Many did not like it and they protested, as people did in generations that followed about the music of Brahms, Berlioz, Wagner and Stravinsky. But the dissonance of one generation becomes the accepted style of the next.

It is these compositions, taken as a group, that make up what music critics and biographers have called Beethoven's "first period." The creative life and work of an artist are indivisible. Still for convenience the idea of three periods and three Beethovens has been created.

Franz Liszt, who as a lad was patted on the head by Beethoven, once said that the "three Beethovens were the Child, the Man, the God." Vincent d' Indy believes that every artist has his three periods, and these he calls "Imitation, Transition and Reflection." It is as though the artist first leaned on others, then walked by himself and finally went far beyond.

Beethoven was influenced by Sebastian Bach, and as we have already seen by Bach's son Emanuel, by Haydn and by Mozart. These influences are present in his first period.

But as the distinguished music historian Alfred Einstein points out, "from the very first his treatment of the matter of music had been poetic and imaginative. The works of the first period speak of the young master's delight in his own strength and of a bold, challenging spirit." And so it was not all "imitation."

This first period of Beethoven's creative life occupied eight years. And in the last of its compositions one can feel the artist groping to free himself from all restraining influences, to free himself so that he can walk alone.

This freedom will come to him suddenly. And from that

moment on we will find Beethoven fully himself and unlike anyone ever born in this world before.

Two events in Beethoven's life took place just before this important change in his creative activity. Both events were highly charged with emotion. And both had a direct influence on what was to follow.

The first was the consuming love for his young pupil Countess Giulietta Guicciardi. She was sixteen and he was thirty-one when they first met. He had his misgivings about marriage because "she is not of my social standing." But still in the full heat of love he dedicated to Giulietta his romantic *Moonlight Sonata*. Here on the opening page of this composition her name has been engraved for all time.

This affair of the heart, which he felt deeply at the time, was certainly a contributing factor to that violent upheaval which was soon to follow. It was this crisis that brought a change to his creative life.

Beethoven at this time was aware of a power and mastery which were welling up inside him. He was searching inwardly for new musical forms. And inwardly he was beginning to hear. New sounds seemed to penetrate the gloom of his silent loneliness.

"I live only in my notes," he wrote to Wegeler. "And when one composition is scarcely finished another is already begun." And toward the end of the year 1801, in another letter to Wegeler he wrote, "If it were not for my deafness, I should long ago have traveled over half the world. . . . Oh, if I were only rid of this affliction, I could embrace the world! . . . No! I cannot endure it. I will take Fate by the throat. It shall not vanquish me. Oh! It is so beautiful to live—to live a thousand times!"

And so it was that in the spring of the year a new hope, a hope of life, came to him.

Having had no benefit from his medical treatments Beethoven changed doctors. Dr. Schmidt, his new doctor, was most encouraging. He felt certain that a quiet place in the country, away from the noise of Vienna, would be beneficial. And so with fresh hope Beethoven took lodging in a place called Heiligenstadt. Today it is a suburb of Vienna, but at that time it was a charming village surrounded by rolling hills, meadows and patches of woodland. Here Beethoven found the peace and the beautiful nature he loved.

He took long walks and, inspired by the lovely countryside, he would pause now and then to mark down a phrase or two of notes in his sketch book which was always at hand. His friends from Vienna often visited him. Some of his pupils also came out to the country for their lessons. The young Ries was one and he has recorded that often they took long walks together. Sometimes Beethoven would sing in his raucous voice, sing a newborn melody and wave his arms wildly to mark the rhythm. The peasants were often frightened by this strange man stamping across the fields and they certainly considered him mad.

On one of these walks Ries heard a shepherd in the distance playing on his homemade flute. He stopped; he listened. But Beethoven heard nothing though he tried for a long while to catch the distant strain of this fleeting sound. "At this," adds Ries, "he became very silent and depressed." This little event made a deep impression on Beethoven.

Sometimes Beethoven's visiting friends, noticing his difficulty, would talk quite loudly. He knew then that his deafness could no longer be kept secret; knew that if the quiet of the country, which Dr. Schmidt had felt would help his hearing, failed, then he must either sink into a well of silence and learn how to live there or . . .

In his mind he turned over all possible alternatives. And by daily brooding over this one tragedy, his mind became morbid. His extreme unhappiness led him to consider mortal release from this crushing bondage—release by suicide.

Time only brought more brooding and to his wretchedness was added despair. And so the summer went. The hope given him by Dr. Schmidt was now abandoned. His hearing did not improve.

To add to his state of depression he received the disturbing news of the marriage of the young countess who he imagined loved him. Now he knew that the affair of her heart was only a flattering fancy. In a vague and unrealistic way he had hoped that her gaiety and warm heart would help him face a bleak world. Now he knew that even this weak hope was gone.

It was then, at the zero hour of his existence, that he wrote that disturbing document which we know today as the "Heiligenstadt Testament." The existence of this document was wholly unknown until after his death when it was found, together with that mysterious letter addressed to his "Immortal Beloved," in a secret drawer of his desk.

This will was written in a close hand on a large folded sheet of paper. The outside is dated, "Heiligenstadt, October 10, 1802." It is addressed to his brothers, "to be read and executed after my death."

This document is important because it reveals his extreme mental and spiritual state and gives us an image of his inner mind. It is important also because of the severity of the crisis through which he passed and because of his thoughts about death. Every sentence is charged with emotional tension.

Oh, you men who think and say that I am hostile, obstinate and misanthropic, how greatly you wrong me! You do not know the secret causes that lie behind the appearance. From my childhood my heart and mind were disposed to the gentle feeling of good will. I was always eager to accomplish great deeds. Only reflect now that for six years I have been suffering from an incurable affliction which has only been aggravated by senseless doctors. Year after year have I been deceived in my hopes for improvement and finally I am forced to face the fact that the illness is lasting. . . . I was compelled at an early date to isolate myself, to spend my days in solitude. . . . I could not prevail upon myself to say to people: Speak louder, shout, for I am deaf. . . . Oh, I cannot do it! You must therefore forgive me if you see me withdraw when I would gladly mingle with you. My affliction is all the more painful to me because it leads to misunderstanding. . . . I must live like an exile. When I do venture near people I am seized with dread that my condition would be discovered. . . . But imagine the humiliation when there was someone standing beside me who heard a flute playing in the distance and I heard nothing, or when someone heard a shepherd sing and, again, I heard nothing. Such occurrences bring me to despair. I would have put an end to my life only for one thing; art held me back. Oh, it seemed impossible for me to leave this world before I had produced all that I was capable of producing. And so I prolonged my wretched existence—truly wretched . . . Patience must now be my guide. I have patience enough. I am determined to hold on until it pleases Fate to cut the thread of life. Perhaps I may get better or perhaps not. I am prepared. . . . Oh God, you can look into my innermost thoughts, you know them, and you know that the love of men and to do good is my ardent desire. Oh, men, when one day you read these words then you will know that you misjudged me.

After some instructions to his brothers, to whom he willed all his worldly goods, as well as the valuable set of four old stringed instruments, made by the famous Italian violin-makers Amati and Guarnieri and presented to him by the generous Prince Lichnowsky, Beethoven continues:

It is my wish that your lives may be better and more free from care than my own. Recommend virtue to your children for virtue alone and not money can bring us happiness. It was virtue that raised me up even in my misery. And it is owing to virtue and to my art that I did not end my life by suicide. Farewell and love one another. . . . Should death come before I have had time to show all my artistic capabilities it will come too soon and I would wish it delayed. Yet, even then I would be satisfied for does not death liberate one from a state of endless suffering? Come when it may I will go forward to meet it.

A few days later, just before Beethoven left for Vienna, he added a heartrending postscript to this Heiligenstadt document:

Thus do I take my farewell of you—and indeed sadly. Yes, that ardent hope which I brought with me when I came here to be cured, at least in some degree, I must now wholly abandon. As the leaves of autumn fall and are withered, so too has my hope been blighted. Almost as I came, I now leave. Even the high courage which has often inspired me during the beautiful summer days, this courage has now left me. Oh

God, grant me at least one day of pure joy, it is so long since true joy has echoed in my heart. Oh, when, Oh, when, Oh, Divine one, shall I feel it again in the temple of nature and of men? Never? No. Oh, that would be too hard.

Thus ends this strange confession, heavily weighted with the talk of suicide and despair. Hope is now, like the autumn leaves, "withered," and once more the idea of Fate is in Beethoven's mind. Fate is now the one who "cuts the cord of life." And even "the high courage which inspired" him during the summer, even this has now deserted him.

But these inspired moments were not lost for Beethoven had carefully recorded them in his notebooks. The pocket notebooks of this summer are filled with musical sketches for the *Second Symphony,* three piano sonatas, three violin sonatas, variations and other compositions. The decks were being cleared. He was no longer content with the old style.

Out of the darkness of his sorrow he was searching the mysterious recesses of the human heart. He was seeking some kind of exalted liberation. A liberation not only for himself but for all mankind.

7

EROICA

Returning to Vienna, Beethoven took up his life as before. He kept secret those thoughts expressed in the Heiligenstadt will. His intimate friends in Vienna still knew nothing of the buzzing and hum in his ears.

He finished several compositions: an oratorio, *The Mount of Olives,* his third *Piano Concerto,* three *Piano Sonatas,* Op. 31, and a *Violin Sonata* which we know today by the name of *Kreutzer.* This sonata, which is almost a double concerto for violin and piano, was written for the brilliant mulatto concert violinist, Bridgetower. The son of an African father and German mother, Bridgetower was known in London as the Abyssinian Prince. At the first performance Beethoven played the piano part. But the sonata was never dedicated to the Abyssinian Prince. It is said they quarreled "over a girl." Instead, the sonata was dedicated to Beethoven's friend, the French violinist, Rudolph Kreutzer. But alas, Kreutzer never liked this violin sonata, which is considered one of Beethoven's best, and he never played it in public. But that is how the name Kreutzer became attached to this now famous sonata.

These compositions, although they were very fine, were still in the old manner and hardly broke new ground. They would be classed in the first period. But they do display a passionate searching for something different.

Czerny records that at this time Beethoven said to his friend the violinist Krumpholz, "I am far from satisfied with my past works. From today on I will turn over a new leaf."

How is one to conquer Fate? How is one to surmount misfortune? Napoleon, a poor cadet from Corsica, had risen to high station. He, too, had been handicapped by poverty and lack of formal education. He, too, believed that Fate was a power and that ordinary mortals could rise to greatness. Was not liberation part of the Revolution? Liberation was in the air. Napoleon's successful campaigns in Italy and Egypt were proof of this new spirit.

In 1798, one of Napoleon's generals, Bernadotte, was sent to Vienna as French ambassador and Beethoven got to know him. The idea of conquering was imbedded in Beethoven's mind. The sword might take kingdoms but music, too, had realms to conquer. Power, he felt, was important. This had been in his mind for some time, for a few years before he had written to his close friend Zmeskall, "The devil take you, I am not at all interested in your moralizing. Strength is the morality of those who distinguish themselves." Did not Napoleon prove that power was all-important? Victory depended upon it. And victory and heroism ride together. For Beethoven, the battlefield was in the heart of man. And he felt himself the conqueror. He was the true hero. He would "take Fate by the throat." Napoleon was only an inspirer, one who proved that this steep road could be journeyed.

The tonal architecture of the *Eroica* or the "Hero Symphony" rose out of this brooding. The power and that burning will to victory is announced in the first movement. This is followed by the wonderful funeral march in which the deathless spirit of the hero marches on. And in the two following movements the spirit, now confident, rushes forward in triumph, a triumph filled with a sublime spiritual joy.

Here, at last, Beethoven had blazed a fresh path. Music was raised to a new glory.

It is related by Beethoven's pupil Ries that, "In writing this symphony Beethoven was thinking of Bonaparte who was then First Consul. Beethoven held him in high esteem and compared him to the great consuls of ancient Rome. Not only I, but many of Beethoven's close friends, saw this symphony on his table, beautifully copied in manuscript. The word 'Bonaparte' was inscribed on top of the title page and 'Ludwig van Beethoven' written at the very bottom, and not another word. How this blank space between these two names was to be filled I did not know. I was the first to tell him the news that Bonaparte had declared himself Emperor, and on hearing this he broke into a rage and cried, 'So he is no more than a common mortal! And from now on he will trample on the rights of man and further only his own ambition. And from now on he will consider himself superior to everybody and become a tyrant!' Beethoven went to the table, snatched the title page of the manuscript, tore it in half and threw it on the floor."

Ries has exaggerated only a little. The manuscript page, which can be seen today, was not torn. But the name Bonaparte has been struck out with a hundred scratches of Beethoven's angry pen.

Napoleon may have inspired the writing of this symphony, but in attempting to describe Napoleon's heroism, his victories, his rise from lowly origin, Beethoven was unconsciously portraying himself. He, too, came from a humble origin. He, too, was short and stocky. Both were little men who felt they had to prove themselves equal to those of average height. Both were filled with ambition and the energy to fulfill these burning desires. Both had outstanding talent. Both believed that there was virtue in power. And both were fully confident and felt themselves masters of their destiny.

In its inner structure the *Eroica* is certainly autobiographical.

The first performance of the *Eroica* did not please the audience. Never before had they heard a funeral march in a symphony. And should not this have been the third movement instead of the second? Besides, the sounds were unpleasant and overdissonant, the modulations and transitions too abrupt. Some thought it much too long. Only a few of the cultured amateurs in Vienna ventured to approve.

It is to the credit and honor of Beethoven's patron, Prince Lobkowitz, that he recognized the rare worth of this symphony. He at once bought the rights of exclusive performance, not for the customary period of a year but for several years. And his orchestra performed the *Eroica* when he desired to honor distinguished visitors. Prince Louis Ferdinand of Prussia, on hearing it played, requested his host, as a special favor, to ask the orchestra to repeat the symphony

from start to finish. From this one might conclude that Prince
Ferdinand had better musical perception than the general
public of Vienna.

The symphony is dedicated to Beethoven's generous patron, Prince Lobkowitz.

The amount of literature written on this single composition
would fill volumes. The *Eroica* is wrapped in myth, fable and
wild supposition. Many music critics have invented theories
to explain different parts of it, and many have searched for
inner intentions. Even Hector Berlioz, who certainly had
keen musical perception, imagined that one section, the last,
described "funeral games around the grave of the warrior,
such as those in the *Iliad*."

In music, images are evoked. They rise from the deep well
of the subconscious. Out of that dark well, which is perhaps
a thousand years old, no two people could bring out similar
images. If they did, it would only indicate that the music was
descriptive, pictorial, and of a mediocre program variety.

But besides images there are other considerations, and
some of these are important. For instance, Alfred Einstein
the distinguished German music historian, states that the first
movement of this symphony "Beethoven was never to surpass,
in which purity of form and depth of poetic intention are
perfectly matched."

And Robert Schauffler, who believes that Beethoven was
"The man who freed music," writes, "When Beethoven
created the *Eroica*, he became a modern Prometheus and
brought to mortal music a hitherto undreamed-of fire . . .
Nothing like the broad lines or the terrific intensities of the
first movement had yet been known. . . . One seems to discern
a heroic form locked in struggle with a huge winged figure,

and to catch the desperate cry: 'I will not let thee go, except thou bless me!' Whatever else from the Master's hand may have aged, these measures are as fresh and luminous with terrible light as the day they were finished."

And again that important turning point in music is expressed by Sullivan in his remarkable study, *Beethoven: His Spiritual Development:* "The first piece of music he composed that has a really profound and important spiritual content is the *Eroica* symphony. . . . The most profound experience that Beethoven had yet passed through was when his courage and defiance of his fate had been followed by despair. He was expressing what he knew . . . Having survived death and despair the artist turns to creation . . . Never before in music has so important, manifold, and completely coherent an experience been communicated."

One more comment may be noted, a comment by Romain Rolland concerning the funeral march in this symphony. He says that it is "in my opinion the modern poem that comes nearest to the elegiac choruses of Greek tragedy; it has the harmonious grace of Sophocles, his natural nobility, his perfection, his serene melancholy." And to this, by way of summing up, he adds, "The *Eroica* is a miracle even among Beethoven's works . . . It inaugurates an era."

Beethoven had kept his word to his friend Krumpholz, "from today on I will turn over a new leaf." And out of the furnace of sorrow emerged a new Beethoven. This is the important Beethoven, the Beethoven who has survived a century and a half. With the *Eroica* begins his second period. And the strains of this Beethoven will sound for many centuries to come.

8

A SHEAF OF MASTERPIECES

BEETHOVEN was fond of contrasts and of opposites. He
composed with a strong sense of black against white,
the serious contrasted with the light, the passionate relieved
by an air of cool detachment.

These were traits found frequently within his works and
sometimes were the characteristics of entire compositions.
For instance, the light, brilliant and sunny *Second Symphony*
was followed by the serious and stirring *Eroica*. And between
the *Eroica* and the tense, dramatic *Fifth Symphony* stands the
light, lively *Fourth Symphony*. Robert Schumann said that
the *Fourth* stands like "a slender Greek maiden between two
Norse giants." Then, too, following the stirring and dramatic
Fifth came that lovely melodic and dreamy *Pastoral,* the
Sixth.

Such contrasts run throughout Beethoven's entire creative
life. And what is true of the symphonies is also true of his
other compositions.

Therefore we are little surprised to find in the piano sonatas that the dramatic *Moonlight,* No. 14, was followed by the melodic and relaxed *Pastoral Sonata,* No. 15. In the same year, 1804, in which Beethoven wrote the epochal *Eroica,* he composed two sonatas which, on the authority of Burk, "reach the highest point of stormy power." These are two of his most famous compositions for the piano, the *Waldstein,* No. 21, and the *Appassionata,* No. 23.

Here again there is evidence of the light and dark in Beethoven. The stress and storm seem overpowering. He was unable to follow the *Waldstein* with that stirring emotional confession, the *Appassionata.* He seemed to require a breathing space. This he provided, no doubt, from his many notebooks. And so "a slender maiden," a little fanciful two-movement sonata, No. 22, is inserted between the two powerful giants.

These two sonatas, especially the *Appassionata,* testify to the condition of the inner man. Now there is strength to meet a tragic fate and a great reserve of power to overcome all forces. The power is one almost of violence. He holds "Fate by the throat." Yet now and again, between the stormy emotional outbursts one feels moments of great tenderness, a heart weeping secretly and in silence.

For emotional turbulence and "stormy power" these two sonatas were never equaled in piano literature. In the years that followed Beethoven composed other sonatas but they were different. They had other qualities.

With the *Eroica* and the *Waldstein* and *Appassionata* sonatas, overflowing with emotional stress, Beethoven ushered in a little musical renaissance. The five years, 1804 to 1809, are years that have never been equaled in all musical history. Masterpiece after masterpiece flowed from his pen. One is

struck by the creative power, by the high plane of imagination, by the energy and by the full range and variety of his
musical output.

Following the two wonderful sonatas and the *Eroica* came
the colorful *Fourth Piano Concerto;* the three much beloved
Razoumowsky Quartets; that beautiful "slender Greek
maiden," the *Fourth Symphony;* the dazzling *Violin Concerto*
and the proud and tragic *Coriolanus Overture.* But this is
not all. These were followed by the dramatic and now world-
famous *Fifth Symphony;* the beautiful and placid *Sixth* or
Pastoral Symphony; the colorful and sweeping *Emperor Concerto* and also two fine trios; a sonata for violoncello and the
well-known dreamlike *Harp Quartet.*

Here were over a dozen masterpieces, created one after the
other during those unparalleled years: 1804 to 1809. And to
these masterpieces still one more was added: the opera
Fidelio.

How many thousands of times have these famous compositions been played in concerts in the century and a half
that has followed? What famous fiddler has not played that
Violin Concerto? What renowned pianist has not played the
Emperor Concerto! And what symphony orchestra has ever
dared to omit the stirring *Fifth* from its repertoire! Of this
symphony alone there are today more than forty LP recordings, by almost as many different orchestras and conductors.

This period of creation was a happy period for Beethoven.
According to his biographer Thayer it was "unquestionably
the happiest" period in the last half of his life. His deafness
was not yet fully upon him. At times he seemed to hear re-
markably well. Little by little his fame had grown. He was
successfully making that great change which he had deter-

mined to make, a change from piano virtuoso to composer. He was still able to play in the great mansions of Vienna before admiring audiences. His friends were devoted. Women loved him. Even with his long complicated process of composition, his slow, sketchbook method of revising, of building theme upon theme, these happy years were most productive.

The work of a creative artist is closely tied to his life. We have already seen how the *Eroica* came into being and how significant was this turning point in the life of Beethoven and in the development of music. And we have already had a word or two to say about the two piano sonatas, supreme examples of Beethoven's emotional turbulence; the *Waldstein* and the *Appassionata*.

But the other masterpieces of this period are so famous, and so Beethovenesque, that a record of his life would hardly be complete without them. Life and work are linked together. To remove one would destroy the other.

The *Razoumowsky Quartets* marked a complete departure in chamber music. It had been six years since Beethoven had written in this form. His previous set of quartets was Op. 18. The Razoumowsky set of quartets was numbered Op. 59. This gap of six years was filled with a great many compositions. Beethoven was forty-one works older.

Count Razoumowsky was the Russian ambassador to Austria. His father, who was half-Cossack, had been one of the lovers of Empress Catherine. The ambassador was married to a sister of Princess Lichnowsky, the wife of Beethoven's generous patron. The count was himself an excellent musician and often played the second violin in chamber concerts. His palace in Vienna soon became the center of musical activity.

But here again, were it not for the quartets that Beethoven wrote for him, Count Razoumowsky's name would today be only a footnote to some obscure page of history.

Beethoven was happy to receive the commission to write these three quartets for Razoumowsky. And since he had already conceived the idea of using folk songs in his intervening themes, he told Czerny that he "pledged himself to weave a Russian melody into every quartet." Some critics say they can trace two Russian melodies in sections of the quartets. But these were so altered, as was everything that Beethoven touched, that they are barely recognizable and of little importance.

What is important is that these quartets are revolutionary in their form. Schauffler calls them "almost orchestral" in their variety and power. "One is sometimes tempted to call them quartet-symphonies." And Burk brings forward their poetic qualities: "The current is broad and deep, vigorously independent, calling forth the full tonal capacity of the four stringed instruments . . . His manipulatory power enormously increased, welds and tightens, liberates, builds. The fancy takes any sort of flight it wills, and is richly various." Burk also believes that the first of the *Razoumowsky Quartets* "is the most widely loved of the Beethoven Quartets."

Although the first quartet may well be "the most widely loved," it is in the slow movement of the third that a very strange and most wonderful influence is felt. With his keen critical perception Sullivan tells about it in the following words: "This movement, indeed, stands alone amongst Beethoven's compositions, and throws an unexpected light upon his imaginative resources . . . This strange movement, as more than one writer has remarked, makes on us the impression of something strictly abnormal. It is as if some racial memory had stirred in him, referring to some forgotten and alien despair. There is here a remote and frozen anguish, wailing over some implacable suffering. This is hardly human suffering; it is more like a memory from some ancient and starless night of the soul. . . . Nowhere else has Beethoven's imagination been exercised in so strange a region."

The *Razoumowsky Quartets* are truly great. But their greatness was slow in being recognized. Some of the musicians who saw the manuscripts of these quartets imagined that Beethoven was playing a joke on them. Some even laughed and said that the music was crazy. Now and then a professional or a talented amateur would admit that some sections had elements of beauty. It was a number of years before the quartets were accepted and played in public concerts. Music that breaks new ground has always had difficulty in establishing itself.

It is interesting to note that the conclusion of each of these three quartets is on a victorious theme. Here the composer is making an autobiographical note. He has brushed aside anguish and human suffering and he gives voice to a different kind of experience, one in which he is master. In the conclusion, the conflict is forgotten and recalled only as an echo.

Three more concerto masterpieces are part of this remarkable period. These are the two final *Piano Concertos:* No. 4; the *Emperor,* No. 5; and the very popular *Violin Concerto.*

Here, too, it had been some years, perhaps five or six, since Beethoven had written in this form. All this time he had been maturing. And now he brought an inspired and unearthly quality to his *Fourth Piano Concerto,* Op. 58—some-

thing of that "ancient and starless night of the soul" which
Sullivan speaks about. Further, the *Piano Concerto* is unusual in its form. Instead of the orchestra introducing the
solo instrument, it is the voice of the piano that introduces
the orchestra.

The slow movement of this concerto, according to Burk,
"has no like in the literature of concertos." It "contains within
its seventy bars a message whose import words cannot convey. It consists of a dialogue between the stringed choir and
the piano . . . It is a recitative and yet it is more. The piano
answers with a melody of indescribable tenderness."

This concerto has become one of the great concert show
pieces of our day. It is tender, melodic and rich in musical
imagination.

The *Emperor*, the last of Beethoven's piano concertos, has
also become a great concert favorite and a display piece for
many brilliant pianists. Beethoven's pupil, Karl Czerny, had
the honor of being the first pianist to perform this concerto
in public.

The composition is dedicated to the Archduke Rudolph.
Because of this dedication and because of its sweeping grandeur, the name "Emperor" has attached itself to this concerto.
But Beethoven had nothing to do with this title and some
critics believe that he would not have approved. Some also
feel that no emperor or archduke has ever been worthy of the
stately grandeur of this music.

In this concerto we find the Beethoven who is able to de-
tach himself from the humdrum world and soar into a rare
mystical realm. Characteristic of his proud "hero" motive—
the assurance that man is master of his fate—the composition

ends with a happy abandon. The clouds part to let the sunshine stream through.

He has kept his word with himself and with mankind. "Fate shall not vanquish me."

The *Violin Concerto*, Op. 61, is the only concerto Beethoven wrote for the violin. It has survived a century and a half and remains today one of the very finest concertos ever written for the violin. No violin virtuoso can omit this composition from his repertoire. Many have risen to fame by their ability to display the warm poetic power in this concerto. The voice of the instrument rings out clearly above the orchestra—the voice of a person alone and removed from the crowd. Phrases are echoed back and forth, but the voice remains clearly apart and fully detached.

The final rondo, like those of the last two piano concertos, rushes into a joyful dance. But even in this dance the solo violin timbre is heard above the orchestra.

In the poetic, sensitive beauty of this concerto Beethoven has enshrined the spirit of the violin.

In addition to the opera *Fidelio*, two more compositions of major importance to the world of music were born in this amazing creative period: the famous C minor, or *Fifth Symphony*, and the *Pastoral*, or *Sixth Symphony*.

The *Fifth Symphony*, which is the world's favorite, is closely related to the *Eroica*. In fact the notebooks show it was begun far back in the years 1800-1801 when Beethoven was brooding about life and death, about his oncoming deafness, about heroism, courage and Fate. Parts were sketched in during that critical summer at Heiligenstadt. It was at this time he wrote, "I will take Fate by the throat. It shall not wholly overcome me."

From the very first four dramatic notes we realize we are not only in the presence of a tragic conflict but that we are ourselves involved. Schindler records that he once asked Beethoven about the four dramatic notes which announce the opening of the symphony, and Beethoven replied, "Thus Fate knocks at the door."

These four notes set the dark tragic mood simply, and as definitely, as the witches do in the opening of *Macbeth*. The witches are prophetic and resigned to Fate, but Beethoven's knock at the door is answered by defiance. This we hear from the very beginning. And this proud defiance is confirmed by the steady progression.

Who is Fate? What cruel force in the universe would destroy the good and the beautiful? Who would bring ruin to the innocent? Could this mysterious Fate be bound to the Creator himself? Had not Beethoven cursed the Creator for "exposing his creatures" to misfortune? Is he daring to battle with God himself!

The theme is clearly sounded. It is, in the words of Sullivan, "Simple and straightforward. But out of this conception Beethoven has composed a movement which is not only interesting, but one of the most masterly pieces of music in existence . . . It is almost unequaled in the impression it gives of inevitable progression. This is one of the very few compositions of which it can be truthfully said that it does not contain an unnecessary bar . . . Beethoven never wrote anything that sounds more 'predestined' from beginning to end . . . At this time in Beethoven's life the issue was simple and clear cut . . . He did not conceive Fate as the blind, cold, indifferent, impersonal order of the universe, but as an enemy."

This enemy is not only Beethoven's enemy. In this conflict we are more than onlookers. We are ourselves involved. And the struggle again takes place in the heart of Man. The victory is a spiritual one and in this we, too, share.

Ideas of heroism, fate, despair, pride, victory and will-to-power are all present in this symphony, as they are in all the creative works of this rich period of Beethoven's existence.

It would have been difficult at this point to imagine or predict what course his future development would take. And yet there is still one more plateau that he will reach. We will then see how all these ideas undergo a marvelous transformation.

The high point of Beethoven's second period is marked by the famous *Fifth Symphony,* in C minor. His power of communication now seems complete. This symphony, says Hector Berlioz, comes "directly and solely from the genius of Beethoven. It is his inmost thought he is going to develop in it, his secret griefs, his concentrated rages, his reveries full of such sad heaviness."

The wonderful thing about it is that the ideas that make up this symphony are universal. They are understood by people of widely different cultures. They are recognized in England, France, Germany, Russia and America. Neither language nor culture is a barrier. The music cuts through. And the emotion of the composer we feel as our own; for in thus recording his emotion so clearly and intensely he has recorded our own emotions.

We begin as detached listeners. We become bystanders. An since our joys and sorrows are involved we are made captive. Soon we are intimately concerned and willingly we participate. The ideas that stem from the composer's narrative we understand. We see fresh vistas of life. We weigh and we revalue. On the dark slate of memory we sponge away our doubts. And without doubts life seems freer and different. We approve. We are satisfied that such changes are good. The very air that we breathe seems filled with a fresh spirit. And this spirit we know can sustain us.

If music can do all this, then it has taken on a new dimension. It has the power to sustain life and help man overcome his doubts and his fears.

Once more Beethoven demonstrates his need for contrast. He is content to leave the fierce struggle with Fate and for his *Sixth Symphony* picture the placid lyrical scenes of nature. This is the nature he understands and loves. And what he sees and feels he describes to us in the *Pastoral Symphony*.

Although Beethoven is opposed to "tone painting" and "program music" and has written a warning line on the manuscript of this symphony: "More the expression of feeling than painting," he has also given descriptive lines to his movements.

The symphony opens with "Awakening of happy impressions in the country." The second movement is "Scene by the brook." This is followed by a "Peasants' merrymaking and thunderstorm." And the final movement he has described as "Shepherd's song and happy and thankful feelings after the storm."

Here again, as in many of his works of this period, we find peace and contentment at the conclusion. Again the clouds part and sunshine streams through.

The entire symphony can well be considered a poem in

praise of nature. And this nature speaks the one language understood by all. We are transported by its serene beauty.

Yet, in spite of its universal language, the *Pastoral* had a hard and long journey before it reached the heart of the public. When first performed it was neither appreciated nor understood. It was many years before this new music became acceptable. Today the popularity of this symphony is boundless.

Beethoven was not a composer for the theater, but still he made an attempt. That which was easy and natural for Mozart and for other composers for the stage, he found difficult. From the very beginning his one opera *Fidelio* was doomed. In the end he spoke of *Fidelio* as my "crown of martyrdom."

The misfortune sprang from Beethoven's temperament. He had a dislike of the popular French and Italian opera of his day. He blamed Mozart for composing music to licentious librettos. Beethoven felt that German opera, serious and ponderous, was the only right kind of opera. Therefore the one opera of Mozart's that had value in his eyes was his German opera, *The Magic Flute*. Beethoven was opposed to light romantic scenes and brought his own prudish morality to the theater.

From the beginning he had trouble finding a suitable libretto. He considered Shakespeare and Greek classical material. In the end he was attracted to a bad libretto written by a French lawyer who, during the Revolution, served as a government official. In this capacity he was witness to a heroic enterprise. This "true story," written up as a "rescue drama," was entitled *Leonora, or Conjugal Love*. The plot

was simple. The beautiful Leonora is determined to rescue
her husband, who has been most unjustly imprisoned. Dis-
guised as a boy, the devoted Leonora becomes a servant in
the home of the jailer. She assumes the name Fidelio. Through
her heroism and the sudden arrival of an important minister
of state the rescue of the innocent husband is accomplished.
So here again we find the hero theme. And here, too, Fate
is cruel to the innocent. And again in the end there are victory and joy. Even the prisoners of the dungeon, a whole
chorus, all are declared innocent and set free!

This libretto suited Beethoven's mood. But the air of freedom which had inspired the libretto was now filled with the
fumes of war. Napoleon's armies were on the march. And
because of this the French dungeon in the libretto was
changed to a castle in Spain!

For two years Beethoven worked hard. Then it became
known that an Italian opera had been made on the same
libretto. Therefore to avoid confusion Beethoven was forced
to change the title from *Leonora* to *Fidelio*.

In the meantime Napoleon's army was crossing Germany
and moving steadily toward Vienna. The sounds of war were
now close. Those who could get out of Vienna lost no time
in doing so.

In these unsettled times the score of the opera was finished
and was ready for rehearsal. But good singers were not to be
found. They had fled from Vienna. Nevertheless, plans for
the performance of the opera, using whatever talent could be
found, were continued.

A week after the victorious Napoleon arived in Vienna the
curtain went up on the first performance of *Fidelio*. The date
was November 20, 1805. The opera house was filled with

French army officers who came only because it offered diversion. They did not understand the music. Beethoven's aristocratic patrons were not in the audience. Even his intimate friends were not there. Beethoven presided at the piano in the orchestra pit. The scenes dragged on and on. The action moved slowly. It was all tedious. The failure was complete. After three performances *Fidelio* was closed down.

Beethoven's friends knew that the failure could not be blamed on the military invasion. The real trouble lay in the opera itself. And so his friends conspired to get Beethoven to make revisions. This was no easy task. "Not one note!" Beethoven shouted.

It was Princess Lichnowsky who, after many hours, finally succeeded in persuading him. She begged him to make *Fidelio* "safe for posterity." She said it would become a memorial to his mother. "Do this for me, for your trusted friend," she urged. In the end his stubbornness melted and he promised to make the suggested changes.

The opera was then compressed into two acts, and improved in many other ways. For this revised version he wrote a new overture which we call today *Leonora No. 3*. The revised opera was performed in the spring of 1806. But again it was not a success.

Eight years later, at the suggestion of the opera house management, *Fidelio* was again revised. At this time Beethoven was much in vogue and the management desired to cash in on his popularity. And now Beethoven was cooperative. Not only was he willing to make changes but he demanded that the libretto be completely rewritten. This was done and the changes helped greatly. "There is hardly a place that I could not have patched," said Beethoven. And he had.

Into this music he poured much affectionate effort. "This is the one that cost me the worst birth pangs, the one that brought me the most sorrow," he told Schindler.

In time *Fidelio* has made its way and slowly it has gained appreciation, perhaps more in Europe than in America. It is now performed periodically by most opera companies throughout the world.

There is a footnote to the history of this opera. During World War II the Opera House in Vienna was badly bombed. But after the war it was rebuilt. And it was with Beethoven's opera *Fidelio* that the new Opera House was inaugurated. This performance took place on November 20, 1955, exactly 150 years after its first performance on the same stage.

With this opera ends that sheaf of masterpieces created, almost one after the other, in the years 1804-1809. Though described briefly, they reveal much about the inner man. But the list is far from complete.

This creative time for Beethoven was full and rich. Besides the *Third, Fourth, Fifth* and *Sixth Symphonies;* the stirring Sonatas; the two last *Piano Concertos;* the *Violin Concerto* and *Fidelio,* Beethoven also composed, in this fertile period, an overture, several trios and the well-known *Harp Quartet.*

There has never been a comparable period in the life of any other composer in all musical history which has given the world such a great number of musical masterpieces.

9

WITHIN THE FURNACE OF CREATION

WHAT goes on inside the creative artist remains mysterious. It is impossible to say where inspiration comes from—what spurs on genius to creation.

Beethoven's method of working was long and involved. Whereas Mozart carried his musical ideas in his head until he felt ready to write them out, and Schubert wrote rapidly on the wings of inspiration, Beethoven depended almost entirely on his notebooks. Here he jotted down his musical ideas, changed them, revised them and wrote them out in a great variety of forms. A crude idea, shaped and altered, grew and grew. Often he would develop musical sketches side by side for several compositions very different in feeling.

His process of composing was indeed slow compared to Mozart, who had written almost fifty symphonies, besides a hundred other major works, in twenty-four years. Slow, too, compared to the creative flights of Schubert who, in a single

year wrote one hundred and fifty songs! It has been related
that when Schubert examined some of Beethoven's notebooks
and saw the amount of labor expended on one theme, he was
appalled.

Some of the sketches remained in Beethoven's notebooks
for years before he felt they were ready for use in a composition. Often ideas came to him when he was out in the country.
Nature was his chief source of inspiration. Next to nature he
found that his music needed to be "fertilized by poetry." But
he regarded nature as visual poetry which he could translate
into music.

The English pianist, Charles Neate, who knew Beethoven
in Vienna, said he had never met a man who took such in-
tense joy in nature. He loved flowers, trees, the clouds, the
sky. He breathed it all in deeply. Nature was nourishment for
him.

Louis Schlösser, a musician from Darmstadt, once asked
Beethoven where he obtained his ideas. Beethoven replied,
"I cannot answer this with any certainty. They come to me
unevoked, often spontaneously and sometimes in association
with other things. It seems to me I could snatch them with
my hands from Nature itself as I go walking in the woods.
Ideas come to me in the silence of the night or in the early
morning, stirred into being by those moods which poets translate into words. These same moods I put into tones; and these
tones resound in my head, singing and roaring with rage
until at last they stand before me in the form of notes."

He also told Schlösser that he often carried his musical
thoughts "a very long time before writing them down. I can
rely on my memory. A theme that has once occurred to me I
am sure not to forget, not even after years have gone by. I

change many things, discard some and try again and again until I am satisfied. Then in my head the development begins. I elaborate on the work in all directions, extending its breadth, its height and its depth. And since I know exactly what I want, the fundamental idea never deserts me. It rises before me. It grows. I see its image from every angle as though it were cast. And only the labor of writing it all out remains. This is usually quickly accomplished when I have the time. But sometimes I am occupied with other work, for very often I work at several compositions at the same time. But I am always sure that one will never be confused with the other."

But often, even when compositions seemed complete, there were times when he felt it difficult to write. "For some time I have been thinking about three other great works," he told a friend. "Much of it is already sketched out, that is in my head . . . Two great symphonies, each different and an oratorio. And these will take a long time, for you see, lately it has not been easy for me to write. I sit and think and think. But it refuses to be put down on paper. I am always terrified of beginning such great works. But once I have started then everything goes along well enough."

Schauffler in his analytical study, *Beethoven: The Man Who Freed Music*, gives a vivid picture of the composer in the country during his last years, as recorded by one of the servants in the house. "At half-past five he was up and at his table, beating time with hands and feet, singing, humming, writing. At half-past seven was the family breakfast and directly after it he hurried out of doors, and would saunter about the fields, calling out, waving his hands, going now very slowly, then very fast, and then suddenly standing still and writing in a kind of pocketbook. At half-past twelve he came into the house to dinner, and after dinner he went to his own room till three or so, then again in the fields until about sunset. At half-past seven he came to supper, and then went to his room, wrote till ten, and so to bed."

Several times the farmer's plowing oxen were frightened by the sudden appearance of this man, singing, shouting and whirling his arms like a windmill. One of the oxen drivers, on seeing this strange figure of Beethoven approach, called out to him, "Go easy there!"

Once in Vienna, during his last years, Beethoven was mistaken for a vagrant and arrested late at night. He was discovered wandering aimlessly in a lonely part of town, humming, talking to himself, waving his arms and marking time with his feet. He was shabbily dressed; in fact Czerny often said that his costume in his last years resembled Robinson Crusoe's. When he told the police he was Beethoven (a name known throughout Vienna) they merely shook their heads. They took him to the police station, where even the captain refused to believe that this strange creature was the great composer. He was held until someone was found who could with certainty identify him.

The outside hulk hardly resembled the wonderful inner glory of genius. But the outer "Robinson Crusoe" shell is not important. This outer picture of the man adds little to the understanding of that process which takes place within the furnace of creation. He was indifferent to appearances. In the heat of creation he was possessed.

10

THE MAN

THE INNER view is the more important one. The spirit of Beethoven lies in his music and not in his words or his actions. Some of the music of his middle period we have already examined. We have also had a glimpse of the outer and superficial aspects of his creative process.

Before proceeding with other events in his life, let us pause and attempt to draw a pen portrait of the man Beethoven. He has announced his genius with the *Eroica*. Destiny has taken him by the hand. Together they march along. He is now approaching the end of that rich middle period which has seen the birth of his *Violin Concerto* and the majestic *Emperor Concerto,* of his famous *Fifth Symphony* and the *Pastoral.*

He is known. He is famous. When a friend asks his address, he replies with pride, "Just write Beethoven, Vienna." It is Czerny's opinion that only Vienna would have put up with his eccentricities, for Vienna was accustomed to artists and devoted to music. Here genius was recognized and respected.

Beethoven once asked Haydn to give him a criticism of himself and his work. Haydn replied, "You make upon me the impression of a man who has several heads, several hearts and several souls."

Haydn must have felt that the inner and outer man were in conflict—that the mortal shell was only a husk that encased the immortal genius.

Beethoven was short and muscular. He was only five feet five inches in height. He was broad, vigorous. In the opinion of Romain Rolland, "He is built of solid stuff well cemented; the mind of Beethoven has strength for its base . . . We see the short stocky body with its great shoulders, the swarthy red face tanned by sun and wind, the stiff black mane, the bushy eyebrows, the beard running up to the eyes, the broad and lofty forehead."

To this description Beethoven's friends have added a number of special features. His broad head was said to resemble the "vault of a temple." His jaws and teeth were so powerful they could grind nuts. He had the muzzle and blunt voice of a lion. His mouth was broad, strong and sensitive. His lower lip protruded slightly and his chin had in it a strong dividing cleft.

The skin of his ruddy face—like the faces of Gluck, Haydn and Mozart—was covered with pockmarks. His eyes were large, dark and alive. Observers do not agree about their exact color. They were black or brown or a dark bluish-gray.

He had a fine torso concealed by his careless clothes. But his thick legs were short in proportion to his body. His hands were broad and red and his fingers short. He had a habit of biting his nails.

Here again we encounter another Beethoven contradiction.

These awkward and clumsy hands could, on the keyboard, produce long rapid runs that dropped notes like pearls falling from a long even string. And the velvet touch of these clumsy fingers had time and time again moved his listeners to tears.

It is hard to believe that such rude hands could have belonged to this piano virtuoso. All accounts, however, agree that he was clumsy in anything that he had to do with his hands, such as dressing himself, eating, or even sharpening a pencil. He never was able to trim his quill pens. His friends cut the quills for him.

His pupil, the pianist Ferdinand Ries, has recorded more details about this difficulty. "Beethoven was very clumsy and awkward in his movements; his gestures were totally lacking in grace. He seldom took up anything without dropping or breaking it. Thus repeatedly his inkwell fell into the piano . . . No piece of furniture was safe with him, least of all a valuable one. Everything was knocked over, dirtied and destroyed. It is difficult to understand how he managed to shave himself. There were frequent cuts on his cheeks. He could never learn to dance in time."

When Beethoven was young he was careless about his dress and slovenly in his appearance. He was poor. He was struggling. After the death of his mother the kindly Madame von Breuning took the raw youth in hand, treating him with the same regard and affection that she gave her own children, and under her guidance his rough manners improved.

When he arrived in Vienna and was trying to make his way as a piano virtuoso, he paid a good deal of attention to his appearance. He dressed carefully and in the fashion of the day. He bought himself black silk stockings and wore fancy cravats and waistcoats.

But as time went on he became more and more absorbed in his work and gave less attention to his appearance. Even during the time he was living as a guest in Prince Lichnowsky's palace he began to be careless about his clothes. He complained to his old friend Dr. Wegeler that dinner in the palace was at four o'clock. "It is desired that every day I shall be home at half-past three so I can put on better clothes and shave myself and all that. I can't stand it!"

And so he had found quarters of his own where the dinner hour would not interrupt his work. In time, as he became more and more possessed by the demon of creation, he grew more and more careless about his appearance. Finally his attire reached that point when Czerny thought he resembled Robinson Crusoe. This was true but only partly true. There were times when he brushed up and made himself presentable. We see him in his later years wearing light-colored trousers and a fashionable dark-blue or bottle-green coat.

His voice was never pleasant. He had a coarse and almost comical Rhine country accent. And as his hearing grew worse his voice became louder and, like the voices of most deaf people, without modulation. Sometimes, walking in the street, he shouted so loud that his friends were embarrassed.

He lived simply and in complete disorder. In the morning he washed himself profusely with cold water. He liked to soak his hands in it. And when he was composing, instead of putting a wet towel to his brow, he poured a pitcher of cold water over his head. Many have reported seeing puddles on the floor close to the piano. In the apartment below (he moved many times and there were many apartments below) the ceilings were ruined.

We already know that much of his furniture was broken and that ink stained the inside of the piano. But let us look around and see what else we can discover.

In his memoirs, a French official named Baron de Trémont records his visit to Beethoven. These vivid pages have been translated by Michael Hamburger and included in his volume, *Beethoven: Letters, Journals and Conversations.* The baron was armed with a letter of introduction, but when he arrived in Vienna he was told that the letter would be of no use as Beethoven was receiving nobody. "He is retiring, sullen and misanthropic." The baron was told that the Empress had asked Beethoven to call on her but that Beethoven replied that he was too busy.

However, the baron decided he would deliver the letter anyway, and records his visit in the following words: "The neighbors showed me where he lived. 'He's at home,' they said. 'Only at this moment he is without a servant. He's always changing them. And because of this it is doubtful if he will open the door.' I rang the bell three times and was just about to leave when a very ugly and evidently ill-humored man opened the door and asked me what I wanted ... He looks at me, takes the letter and motions that I should enter. His apartment, I think, consists of but two rooms. The first contained an enclosed alcove—in which his bed stood— so small and dark that he had to perform his toilet in the next room or in the drawing room. Imagine all that is most filthy and untidy; puddles on the floor, an old grand piano covered with dust and piled high with music, printed and in manuscript. Beneath the piano, and I do not exaggerate, was

an unemptied chamberpot. The little walnut table next to
the piano was evidently accustomed to having the contents
of the inkwell spilled over it. A mass of pens encrusted with
ink—and more musical scores. The chairs, most of them straw
chairs, were covered with plates full of the remains of last
night's supper and with clothes, etc. . . .

"I spoke only a broken German, but I understood it a little
better. Nor was his French any more fluent. I expected him
to dismiss me as soon as he had read the letter . . . But I
was quite astonished when he continued to look at me, put
down the unopened letter on the table and offered me a
chair. I was even more astonished when he began to talk. He
asked about my uniform, my profession, my age, the purpose
of my journey; whether I was a musician and whether it
was my intention to spend more time in Vienna. I replied
that Reicha's letter would explain all this much better than
I could explain it myself. 'No, no, speak,' he said. 'But speak
slowly for I am very hard of hearing, but I shall understand
you'. . . . my bad German and his bad French produced the
strangest of mixtures. But we understood each other. The
visit lasted three-quarters of an hour and he invited me to
visit him again.

"I left prouder than Napoleon when he entered Vienna:
I had conquered Beethoven."

The baron returned a number of times and got to know
Beethoven, who even played for him. "Beethoven's improvisations," wrote the baron, "were certainly the deepest of all
my musical experiences. I am quite sure that no one who has
not heard him improvise freely and spontaneously can wholly
grasp the vast extent of his talent. Sometimes, quite on the
spur of the moment, he would say to me, after striking a few

chords, 'I can't think of anything, let's leave it for another time.'" Then they would talk about philosophy or religion and often "about Shakespeare, his idol."

Among Beethoven's books, besides Shakespeare, were the Bible in French and Latin, the Apocrypha, Homer, the Fables of La Fontaine, Thomas à Kempis, the poetry of Goethe, Schiller and Klopstock, Plutarch's *Lives*, Kant's *Theories of the Heavens*, and twenty volumes of classical tales for children which he had bought when his young nephew Karl came to live with him. He was also acquainted with several works of Oriental mystical philosophy. He copied out pages from these and kept the mystical and bewildering words before him on his desk.

Beethoven had a complete set of Klopstock, a second-rate romantic and pessimistic German poet. For many years Klopstock served to inspire him, for Beethoven felt that music needed to be "fertilized by poetry." But when his values of life began to change, he found Klopstock depressing. He once explained it all to a friend. "Goethe has killed Klopstock for me. I gave myself up to him for many years— when I took my walks and at other times. . . . I did not always understand him. . . . Why should he always want to die? . . . That will come soon enough. . . .But Goethe—he lives and he wants us all to live. That is the reason he can be composed. Nobody else can be so easily composed as he." Thus he gave up the minor poet Klopstock and found his chief inspiration in Homer, Goethe and Schiller.

Goethe's passionate plea for life, as summed up in the first part of *Faust*, was not published until 1808. But many of Goethe's previous works were approaching this philosophy.

By the year 1808, Beethoven had already composed his *Fifth* and *Sixth* symphonies, besides his *Razoumowsky Quartets* and other works that in music embraced a similar life spirit or credo. Thus the publication of the first part of *Faust*, and this was an important literary event, merely confirmed his inner convictions. The march of life was to him a noble one, and all difficulties could be surmounted. In this triumph over difficulties he found the spiritual glow of life.

Many biographers have believed that because of the failure of his opera *Fidelio* Beethoven had given up all idea of writing for the theater. This is hardly so for his sketchbooks include rough musical notations for two large and important operas: *Faust* and *Macbeth*.

As his deafness increased and he withdrew into himself, he turned more and more to books for solace. In his extreme loneliness he searched for words. He loved the dramatic, tales of conflict and stories of heroes. As for poetry, his tastes were never highly refined. Second-rate romantic verses remained to the end his main musical "fertilizer," though often, as he himself confessed, he did not quite understand them. But he did not require complete understanding. Words were ever in the way. It was the spirit and emotional sense that gave fuel to his creative furnace.

Beethoven's living conditions became more and more disordered. Even though he had two fine pianos and priceless violins, a rare cello and other instruments of great value, still his rooms, filled with confusion, dirt and broken furniture, always resembled a slum. When his deafness became more acute, even the pianos were badly neglected. They were out

of tune and at times strings were broken, buzzing and clank-
ing as he played.

He was always proud to the point of arrogance. As he
grew older he became irritable, ill-mannered, short-tempered
and intolerant. He was oversensitive and quarreled with little
reason. He quarreled with his best friends, his patrons, his
publishers, and his relations. Often he regretted his violent
and impulsive actions and tried to make amends on the
following day.

He once quarreled with the young pianist Hummel, who
had been a pupil of Mozart. Hummel was devoted to Beethoven, yet one day Beethoven wrote him a most insulting
letter—written in the third person: "He is not to come to see
me again. He is a treacherous dog and may the Reaper take
all treacherous dogs. Beethoven." The cause for this abusive
letter is not known. But on the folowing day, in deep remorse,
Beethoven wrote, "Dearest Nazerl, you are an honest fellow
and I now see you were right. Come, then, to me this afternoon. You will find Schuppanzigh here also, and we two will
bump, thump and pump you to your heart's delight. A kiss
from Your Beethoven, also known as Mehlschöberl." Schuppanzigh was first violinist in Lichnowsky's quartet and a good
friend. A *Mehlschöberl* is a Viennese pancake, or dumpling,
which is added to beef broth.

But many of Beethoven's quarrels were not easily patched
up. As for his relatives, he brought several lawsuits against
his sister-in-law. And he opposed his brother, the apothecary,
who wanted to buy a house and shop in Linz. But in this his
brother went ahead anyway without Beethoven's help or
blessing, and in a very short time he secured a contract to

supply medicines to the French army stationed in the neigh-
borhood. By this move he established himself, and prospered.

Early biographers of Beethoven, assuming that genius was
always misunderstood, sympathized with Beethoven and
concluded he was always right and the others always in the
wrong. But a detached study of the documents proves clearly
that it was Beethoven who was usually at fault.

His irritability and his quarrelsome nature were due to a
combination of things: bad health, approaching deafness,
lack of appreciation, insecurity, and impatience. His complete ignorance of the world, its social forms and conventions,
often caused him to take offense where none was intended.
He was easily wounded. Sometimes his wounds healed
quickly and sometimes he carried the scar for years.

In the main, Beethoven was honorable, but there were
several times in his life when his publishers accused him of
dishonesty. Once he accepted money for a new work, but
after composing the new work he sold it to a rival publisher
and gave an old, inferior composition to the publisher who
had advanced the money for a new work. And once he sold
the same work to four publishers! On the other hand, his
artistic integrity made him refuse a £100 advance from the
Philharmonic Society of London for a symphony to be written in his earlier style. The offer came at a time of need, yet
he was deeply offended and refused to compromise with his
art. He once told the poet Matthison, "The greater one's progress in art, the less one is satisfied with one's earlier works."

In time, as Beethoven's hearing became worse, he became
suspicious. He once complained to a friend that he believed
his servants were stealing food from his kitchen, and that the

young maid must have grievances against him, for when she brought up a basket of firewood her face looked cross.

He was often intolerant and complained about the great number of amateur musicians in Vienna who gave lessons, put on concerts and set themselves up as arrogant critics of music.

Yet the amateurs, as well as the professionals in Vienna, recognized his greatness and tolerated his *raptus*, his brooding and his eccentric manner.

Later on he estranged many by his uncompromising demands and his hypochondria. Czerny, who was ever devoted, was convinced that only Vienna could have tolerated Beethoven and his peculiarities: "It is doubtful if he would have been left so undisturbed in any other country. It is true that as an artist he had to fight cabals, but the public was innocent in this. He was always marveled at and respected as an extraordinary being, and his greatness was suspected even by those who did not understand him."

He was too great to be ignored and too eccentric to be loved by those who did not know him.

But with all his faults he had a happy faculty of making friends. In spite of his irritability and stubbornness and bad manners he held his friends captive. They did everything they could for him. They were devoted. And some of them, including Czerny, Hummel, Stephan von Breuning and Schindler, were with him from his first days in Vienna to the very last.

A picture of Beethoven would hardly be complete without a word about his handwriting. He wrote with a bold, energetic hand and with a marked slope and flourish. He confessed in a letter to a friend that he found it difficult to express himself in words and often delayed writing because of this. In time impulsive impatience made his handwriting difficult to decipher. He often made fun of his illegible script and added by way of excuse, "Life is too short for me to paint letters on notes. And notes more carefully penned would hardly relieve my poverty."

As the years wore on, his script took on the expressive traits of good calligraphy and presented that free flowing motion known and prized by the Orientals as "grass writing."

His music manuscripts are revealing. In his first period in which his music related to the reality of life, the notes are carefully scribed, orderly and legible. In his second period, in which he looked out from the world of reality into a loftier and more spiritual realm, the notes are rushed onto the page with energetic impulse and with a repeating rhythm, as though they were a series of arcs brushed in by the wing of a bird. Here an impatient driving force and no hesitation can be noted.

In his last period, in which he left the world completely behind and was concerned only with the spiritual aspects of life, his musical script grew into a strange flowing shorthand in which brief signs and symbols expressed the longhand of the ideas. The ideas themselves were wild expressions, highly original and perhaps containing within them a trace of spiritual revelation.

It was up to his music copyist to decipher this code and do it correctly, for Beethoven would stand no trifling by a scribe. Nor would he tolerate any suggestions. To one copyist who offered suggestions he wrote, "Dirty Scribbler! Stupid Fellow!

Correct the blunders which you have made in your ignorance, insolence, conceit and stupidity. This would be better than to try to teach me. It is as if a sow attempted to give lessons to Minerva!"

11

BEETHOVEN AND GOETHE

Toward the end of that very productive period—a time that began with the *Eroica* and included the *Appassionata*, the famous *Fifth Symphony*, and many other masterpieces—Beethoven felt that Vienna was unappreciative. He grumbled about the stupidity of the public and because his application for a court position was completely ignored. Because of all this he said he would be glad to leave Vienna if some suitable position were offered him. He was known abroad. His name was now linked with Mozart and Haydn. Masterpieces flowed from his pen, and yet in Vienna he felt himself insecure.

Thus it happened that in the fall of 1808 an emissary from the King of Westphalia called on Beethoven and offered him the position of *Kapellmeister* of the court of Cassel. In this post he would receive 600 ducats in gold and he would have "nothing to do but play occasionally for the King and conduct his chamber concerts."

The King of Westphalia was Jérôme Bonaparte, the

youngest member of that ugly Bonaparte tribe. He was twenty-three years old and had been married to an American girl, Elizabeth Patterson. But this had not fitted in with his brother's plans of world domination, and so Napoleon dissolved the marriage and forced Jérôme to marry a German princess, Catherine, daughter of the King of Württemberg. Then Napoleon crowned his brother King of Westphalia.

The new king had been on his throne only one year when he sent his emissary to Beethoven. His young court needed building up. Beethoven was already acknowledged in many parts of Europe as the greatest living musician. In one stroke the court of Cassel would gain distinction and attract the cultural attention of Europe. His offer was a generous one and one that Jérôme knew would tempt Beethoven. An annual salary of 600 gold ducats would lift the weight of insecurity and allow Beethoven freedom to compose.

But some of Beethoven's friends, learning of this offer, conspired to keep him in Vienna. It was the Countess Erdödy who persuaded the Archduke Rudolph to join with Prince Lobkowitz and Prince Kinsky in offering Beethoven an annual grant of 4,000 florins, the equivalent of Jérôme Bonaparte's 600 gold ducats, to remain in Vienna. These donors wanted Beethoven to have free time to devote to his creative work and promised to continue this annuity until Beethoven accepted a court position as *Kapellmeister*. The contract was signed on March 1, 1809.

The money, added to the little that dribbled in from publishers, was sufficient for his needs. In one stroke three generous and aristocratic patrons removed petty anxiety. Beethoven was now free and he was happy.

✻   ✻   ✻

In the following year, 1810, an attractive young woman by the name of Bettina Brentano sought out Beethoven and wrote a long and wonderful letter about him to Goethe. In this year the petite Bettina, who was also called Elisabeth, was twenty-six years old, but she looked younger and passed herself off for twenty-one. She was cultured, articulate, and eager to know great personages. She was a tufthunter. But her worst trait was that she was very careless with the truth. Her words are not always to be trusted. Nevertheless she had gained the acquaintance of the great German poet Goethe and now had thrown herself at the feet of Beethoven.

To Goethe she wrote, "When I saw this man, of whom I wish to speak to you, I forgot the whole world . . . It is Beethoven of whom I now speak. . . . Like clockwork, the whole human activity moves within him, he alone creates the undivine and this flows freely from his own depths. What does worldly intercourse mean to him? He is at work at his sacred craft before sunrise. And after sunset he is still at work, forgetting to nourish his body. His spirit is carried over the banks of our flat lives on wings of ecstasy.

"He himself has said, 'When I open my eyes, I must sigh, for what I see is contrary to my religion, and I must despise the world which fails to understand that music is a higher revelation than the whole of wisdom and philosophy. Music is the wine that incites us to new creation and I am the Bacchus who presses this glorious wine for mankind and makes them drunk spiritually. When they are sober again they will have fished up much from the sea and this they bring with them to dry land. I have no friends. I must live alone with myself. Yet I know well that God is nearer to me than he is to other artists; I associate with Him without fear; I have always recognized and understood Him and have no fear for my music—it can meet no evil fate. Those who understand it must be freed by it from all the miseries that bow men down.'

"All this Beethoven said to me when we met for the first time. I was filled with reverence for the friendly manner in which he received me. I was also astonished, for I had been told he was most retiring and had few conversations with anyone. People were afraid to take me to his home, and so I had to look him up alone. He has three different apartments. . . . I entered unannounced, he was seated at the piano. I told him my name and he kindly asked me if I would like to hear a song he had just composed. He then sang *Kennst du das Land?* 'It's beautiful, isn't it?' he said with enthusiasm. 'Very beautiful.' He was pleased with my approval. 'Most people are moved by something that is good, but not if they are artists by nature. Artists have fire in them and they don't weep.'

"He escorted me home and it was on the way that he said all these fine things about art. But he raised his voice so much that people in the street stopped suddenly and I needed courage to continue. He spoke with great passion . . .

"Yesterday he accompanied me to a garden in full bloom, all the hothouses were open. The scent was intoxicating. Beethoven stood still in the oppressive heat of the sun and said, 'Goethe's poems exercise great power over me not only by their content but also by their rhythm. His language stimulates me and induces in me a mood to compose. . . . And so in a spirit of enthusiasm I must discharge melody in all directions. I pursue it, passionately, and catch up with it. I see it escape me and vanish. . . . Then I capture it once more with renewed passion and now I cannot bear to part with it but must expand it with ecstasy in all its modulations. And so at the last moment I triumph over the first musical idea. You see, that's a symphony. And surely music is the joining mediator between the life of the spirit and the life of the senses. I should like to speak about this to Goethe. Do you think he would understand me? Melody is the sensual life of poetry.

" 'Speak to Goethe about me and tell him to listen to my symphonies. Then he will agree with me that music is the only entrance to the higher world of knowledge which understands mankind but which mankind fails to understand. A certain rhythm of the spirit is needed in order to grasp the essence of music . . . The more the spirit takes of the sensuous nourishment from music the more will the mind develop and understand the meaning of music . . .

" 'Music is the electric soil in which the spirit lives, thinks and creates. . . . Every genuine creation of art is free and more powerful than the artist himself and through its very existence returns to the divine. With man it has only this in common: it bears witness to the meditation of the divine that lives in him . . .

" 'Write to Goethe about me . . .' "

Bettina Brentano says she wrote all this down in the evening, as soon as she returned to her home. It was thus fresh in her mind.

The next day when she saw Beethoven she read him what she had written. "Did I say all that?" he asked. "Well, in that case I must have been in one of my *raptus*."

He looked at what she had recorded, crossed out several lines and wrote in some other words.

Some critics have thought that Bettina allowed her imagination to wander freely. And since it is know that she was, at times, careless with facts, in a vain desire to glorify herself, and even invented things that had never happened, this document has been under suspicion.

But even allowing for exaggeration and a literary elegance Beethoven certainly did not possess, this still contains ideas about life and music that Beethoven has been known to express. And some authorities—Thayer, Bekker, Rolland and Schauffler—agree that in the main the substance of the material is Beethoven's. We already know that Beethoven felt that poetry was a "fertilizer" for his music and that often, although he did not grasp its meaning, the words and rhythm evoked in him a desire to create. These ideas restated in this document help give it authenticity.

Regardless of the fact that one biographer has called Bettina a "lascivious" meddler and "the crowning bloom in the hothouse of pseudo-Romanticism," she still has one great distinction to her credit. In the words of Schauffler, "This strange young girl was the first person to discover and express on paper the true greatness of the Beethoven we know today." Sullivan considers Bettina's account of great importance for it is "almost the only evidence we have as to Beethoven's conception of the function of music." This suggests "that Beethoven regarded art as a way of communicating knowledge about reality." Thus Sullivan concludes that we are confronted with "a theory which, if true, means that art has a significance very much more important than that usually attributed to it. Art must rank with science and philosophy as a way of communicating knowledge of reality." And so today, one hundred and fifty years later, we discover that Beethoven was projecting ideas that are now part of that rare subject, the philosophy of aesthetics. Here we have the first hints of the "compelling emotional force" of art, and the idea that experience is a field that has dimensions, and creative works are great in accordance with the extent and quality of the field of experience. We know, of course, that the historical accident, which we call language, still retains its marked skeleton, because of the poverty of its lowly origin. But the language of music is free of this poverty.

These are only a few of the suggestions which this very important document projects into our modern philosophical realm. Year by year the importance grows. We recognize today that experience is contained in the essence of music and that this experience, which is capable of becoming part of music, is more and more part of our own existence.

But how about Goethe? Did he reply to Bettina's letter? Yes.

But the reply was cool and suspicious. He believed that "incongruities" might be discovered in Beethoven's statements. He was ready to admit that "a layman must respect the statements of one possessed by a daemon, and it matters not whether he speaks from feeling or from knowledge for here the gods are at work scattering seed."

He assured Bettina that he would be very glad to meet Beethoven. Perhaps she could persuade him to journey to Karlsbad where he himself went every year for the baths, and then he would have the "leisure to listen to him." To this he added that it would be very nice if Beethoven would send him the two songs he had composed to words Goethe had written, but that they should be "very clearly written. I am most eager to hear them. It is one of my greatest pleasures."

This last was perhaps only complimentary and not quite
sincere. Goethe, like many literary men, had little musical
taste or understanding.

Beethoven was highly pleased to have the attention of Germany's foremost poet, the leader of the Romantics and foun-
der of that short-lived literary movement called *Sturm und
Drang*. This movement, which attracted writers of the time,
had in it boldness and an awareness of anxiety. But the
anxiety was mainly of a personal nature and did not include
the larger problems of mankind or today's awareness of a
social conscience. Goethe's *The Sorrows of Werther*, an early
romantic autobiographical novel, was part of this movement.

Goethe was twenty-one years older than Beethoven, who
was a child when *Werther* was published and became a
literary sensation in Europe. Although all his life Beethoven
held the name Goethe in great reverence, *Werther* did not
inspire him. He could find no heroism in its self-pity. But he
was fully captivated with the tragedy *Egmont*. The hero of
Egmont is a young man who struggles with glorious courage
against the forces of Fate. He is misunderstood and yet he
marches on. He is a champion of liberty and independence
and meets his death on the scaffold in defense of these principles. Through his sacrifice his people take courage. This was
the kind of "hero stuff" that Beethoven admired.

The times were changing and *Egmont* was a revolt against
the *Sturm und Drang*. In a strong tragic drama it expressed
new ideas about liberty, humanity and society. *Egmont* first
appeared in 1788, a year before the French Revolution began.

Beethoven was attracted to *Egmont* for two reasons. It
presented a republican point of view which he admired. To

champion freedom in Beethoven's time was to open oneself
to the charge of treason. Yet Beethoven, who had risen from
lowly station, believed in equality and felt himself, because
of the force of his talent, equal to any king.

There was another reason why Beethoven was enamored
with *Egmont*. He saw himself in the role of the misunderstood hero. This was his life also. This was his own struggle
with Fate. And death on the scaffold was nothing compared
to the agonizing daily torture of his deafness.

He refused to accept any money for writing the incidental
music to *Egmont*. This was a labor of love.

Now Beethoven took courage and wrote directly to the
great poet Goethe. He wrote to thank him "for the long
time" he had known him, "since my childhood." Also, that
he was pleased to hear from their mutual friend Bettina that
they might look forward to meeting. "I can only approach you
with the greatest reverence, with an unspeakable, profound
feeling for your fine creations. You will soon be receiving the
music for *Egmont*. . . . I should be very pleased to have your
judgment of it, and even your adverse criticism."

It was in this way that the music of *Egmont* came into
being. Once more Beethoven put into sound the courage to
surmount Fate and march toward the goal of triumph.
Schauffler sums it up with the line, "All of the *Egmont* music
bears the stamp of greatness."

Although Bettina fascinated Beethoven—she was sympathetic
to him, thus enabling him to talk about his art and its inner
problems—she was not at all in love with Beethoven. And he
was not in love with her. She was proud to receive his atten-
tions. She knew she was attractive and she was determined

to use all her charms to stir up a fever of inspiration in the Master. But she also had other designs. She was really in love with Goethe, whom she was eager to meet, and was using Beethoven and his admiration for Goethe to further her correspondence with the poet.

After leaving Beethoven she went to Goethe. Her first sight of the poet caused her to swoon. "I stretched my hands toward him, I believe," she wrote to her mother. "I was soon conscious of nothing more. Goethe clasped me suddenly to his heart . . . He carried me into his room, and placed me opposite to him on the sofa." After a short time on the sofa, "I flung myself on his neck. He took me upon his knee and pressed me to his heart. . . . I fell asleep on his breast, and when I awoke began a new life."

One of Goethe's biographers, Hayward, comments on this passionate romance, "If we are to believe her story . . . Goethe encouraged and returned, or pretended to return, her passion, till he got tired of her." Bettina played her cards carefully. To her diary she secretly confessed she was "like a spider" weaving a web around Goethe, "ensnaring him softly, softly . . ." And she made Beethoven part of her scheme.

She had succeeded in fascinating Beethoven and she gave Goethe a running account of her encounters with him. She insisted that Beethoven was a musical genius. But Goethe, who had no judgment on music, was not convinced.

He was inclined to side with his friends, who felt that Beethoven was an innovator, who overdramatized trifling musical ideas.

In the meantime the music for *Egmont* was delayed by the publisher and by the time it reached Goethe he was already weary of Bettina—this bold intellectual child who had thrown herself at his feet. And before a meeting could be brought about between Goethe and Beethoven, Bettina departed and was married to the young man to whom she had long been engaged.

But about a year later the two men of genius did meet at Teplitz, where Beethoven had gone for his health.

Goethe was quick to feel the strength and unique genius of Beethoven. They took a long walk, exchanged ideas, and in the evening Beethoven played for him. But after this first encounter the friendship did not ripen.

There were good reasons for this. In the first place, Beethoven's deafness made conversation awkward. Goethe's lack of musical appreciation prevented him from understanding that other language in which Beethoven was articulate.

It has been said that Beethoven derived more from this brief encounter than Goethe, for his veneration of the poet had endured many years and was indestructible. As for Goethe, he was stiff, cold, calculating, and brushed off Beethoven's most moving playing with such formal remarks as "most charming." Goethe did not warm up to a closer friendship. But there is still more to be said.

Both men had begun by admiring Napoleon. They had admired him because he had risen from a low station. Both Goethe and Beethoven had broken those solid European bonds of caste. They had admired Napoleon when he was the son of the revolution, the liberator of oppressed countries, and the First Consul. But the moment he crowned himself Emperor, Beethoven in anger took Napoleon's name off the cover of the *Eroica*. However, Goethe continued to remain friends with Napoleon and was even greatly flattered by an invitation to visit the Emperor.

This visit took place in the fall of the year 1808, when Napoleon was in his full glory. Goethe came forward and stood before the Emperor, who slowly looked him over and finally said, "You are a man!" This was most complimentary, but then the arrogant Corsican proceeded to deliver a lecture on *Werther* and on literature. Goethe stood and listened patiently. Some time later, at the official ball, Napoleon drew Goethe aside to tell him that he was astonished that so great a literary genius should admire Shakespeare instead of the true dramas of history, and suggested that the death of Caesar would make a suitable subject. Goethe listened and bowed politely.

Here lies the difference between Goethe and Beethoven, who would never have listened in silence to a Napoleon talking out of his emotionally charged ignorance. This gap between the two artists was deep and Beethoven felt it when they met in the fall of the year 1812. "Goethe is too fond of the atmosphere of the courts, more than becomes a poet," he wrote to his music publisher. As for Goethe, he considered Beethoven "an utterly untamed creature."

And at that moment where was the dazzling Napoleon? He had just arrived in Russia, and in this very month found Moscow destroyed by fire. Soon would begin that famous retreat that would lead to his devastating defeat and finally to his exile in Elba. During this exile the princes, kings and emperors of Europe were to hold a Congress in Vienna. Here Beethoven would play his part. Beethoven—but not Goethe.

There was still another important difference in their humanitarian outlook and in their views of liberty. Goethe was twenty-seven when the American Revolution fired the shot heard round the world. He was forty when the French Revolution began, and he was eighty-one when, in 1830, Europe was again in the convulsions of revolution. He said that this particular revolution was a pity, for it would delay the meeting of the French Academy of Science! He did not think that man should strive for liberty and he said he much regretted the impulse that carried Byron to Greece. He liked aristocracy and was indifferent to the rights of man.

Except for *Egmont*, and one or two minor verses, he was at no time in his long and successful literary existence concerned with the emergence of man from his centuries of heavy bondage. In short, he lived a long life and never dipped his pen to aid his fellow men. This is the charge that humanity places against him. And this is what Beethoven reacted against. It is why *Egmont*, of all Goethe's voluminous writings, is the only one for which Beethoven wrote a musical score.

To all of this there is a little postscript. Goethe tried hard to fathom the meaning of music. He was aware of his great deficiency. In the autumn of 1830, about three years after Beethoven's death, Goethe persuaded Felix Mendelssohn to give him "music lessons." Mendelssohn came to his home every day and played on the piano for an hour. He began with the earliest music and gave him examples in historical order. When he finally came to contemporary music, he hesitated before launching upon Beethoven, and even apologized. But when he played the score of the C minor Symphony (the *Fifth*) Goethe remarked, "That causes no emotion. It is only astonishing and grandiose." He was silent and thought about it for a brief time, then revised his judgment. "That is very grand, and wild enough to bring the house down about one's

ears. And imagine what it must sound like when it is played
by a full orchestra!"

This appreciation of Beethoven came too late to do Beethoven any good. Had it come earlier it would have glad-
dened his heart.

12

END OF A PERIOD

W HILE Napoleon was retreating from Moscow in the fall of 1812, Beethoven was encountering some personal difficulties. Having finished his *Seventh Symphony* he started his *Eighth*. This he composed quickly. In about four months he had finished it, as we know from his inscription on the manuscript: "Linz, in the month of October, 1812."

It is surprising that he was able to finish this *Eighth Symphony* while in Linz. For what happened there was most disturbing.

He had come to Linz filled with moral indignation. He had learned that his brother Johann, the druggist, had a mistress whom he intended to marry.

The girl, Therese Obermeyer, could not really be called a loose woman. Johann had rented a floor of his large building to a doctor, his wife and his wife's sister. Therese was the sister. In time she became Johann's housekeeper. Beethoven assumed she was an evil woman who desired to marry his brother. He was determined to stop the marriage.

After a violent quarrel with his brother, Beethoven launched upon a headstrong and tactless procedure. He went to the police and denounced Therese Obermeyer as a loose and immoral woman. He demanded that she should be returned to Vienna by force if she did not leave Linz by a certain day. He managed to obtain this order in writing from the police.

But before the time expired for Therese to leave, Johann married her. And so the very result Beethoven was eager to avoid had been brought about. This is perhaps a fair example —there are others—of Beethoven's complete lack of understanding of normal people and of simple affairs of the world.

But the marvel remains: how, during all this violent emotional upheaval, was he able to finish that light, flowing and lyrical, heart-warming *Eighth Symphony?*

Returning to Vienna, he encountered more trouble. His other brother, Karl, was taken ill and out of his small income Beethoven helped to support him and his wife and child. He had little liking for Karl's wife for he thought that she also belonged to what he had called that "tribe" of bad Viennese women. Yet he provided for Karl's family and at times it was a sacrifice. Because of his deafness, he had ceased to perform, either in public or in private.

Beethoven was careless about money. For a number of years he had received fair sums from music publishers. But in recent years he had not been writing much and the fees declined. Through necessity he lived mainly on the income provided by his patrons. He tried to make this suffice until other payments could arrive.

But now there was more trouble. The payments were unavoidably reduced.

Because of war, Napoleon's war in Europe, Austrian money suffered inflation and dropped to one fifth its value. The contract Beethoven had made with the Archduke Rudolph, Prince Kinsky and Prince Lobkowitz, about three years before, called for an annual payment of 4,000 florins. When the inflation began, the Archduke Rudolph, in all fairness, increased the amount of his contribution to make up the difference. But the other two princes were not in a position to do so, for the war had reduced their financial reserves.

To add to the difficulty, in November 1812, Prince Kinsky was killed by a fall from a horse and his payments were tied up until the estate could be settled. This proved to be a matter of years.

Troubles, of course, ride in battalions. Prince Lobkowitz went bankrupt. Only the Archduke was able to contribute his share, and to his honor it must be said that he paid a sum equal to the promised amount before it suffered inflation.

No wonder we find Beethoven's friend, Louis Spohr, writing at this time to ask Beethoven why he had not seen him in their usual restaurant for lunch. "You were not ill, were you?" he asked anxiously. And Beethoven replied, "No, but my boots were; the one pair I have gave out and I was under house arrest."

His good friend Madame Nanette Streicher (she and her husband were devoted to Beethoven) records that during this period she found Beethoven "in the most desolate state as regards his physical and domestic requirements. He did not have a single good coat, and not a shirt that was whole." She did what she could to keep his establishment running.

She gave instructions to the servants and periodically in-spected the kitchen books. It was to Nanette Streicher that he once complained that he suspected the servants of steal-ing food from the kitchen.

Music was the tie that linked the Streichers to Beethoven. It was a very strong tie with roots deep in piano tradition.

To begin with, Nanette's father, Johann Andreas Stein, was a piano builder who developed the instrument and set it on its modern path. He was a friend of Mozart and Mozart once said, "I prefer Stein's [pianos], for they damp off the resonance much better . . . I can let my finger remain on the key and the moment I lift it the sound ceases and it does not jangle disagreeably."

Nanette first performed for Mozart when she was eight years old. In a letter to his father, Mozart ridiculed her posi-tion at the piano. "She is seated right up toward the treble." But later he gave her lessons and her position was improved. In time she married Andreas Streicher, a dear friend of the poet Schiller. Andreas came into the piano business, which he inherited at the death of Stein, his father-in-law.

These Viennese pianos, while they presented an advance-ment in piano design, were still delicate and retained some-what the tonal flavor of their ancestors, the clavichords and harpsichords. This was suitable for the easy flowing tech-nique of Mozart or Haydn or Clementi. But it was unfit for the weight and power of the new Beethoven music. That is why we read in so many accounts that Beethoven's piano was out of tune and its strings were broken. Some years later, in 1818, Beethoven received a present of an English Broadwood piano and this he found more powerful. For this piano he wrote his strenuous *Hammerklavier Sonata.*

Piano action was later improved in France and in the United States. The cast-iron frame—designed to take the high tension off the strings, away from the soundboard and frame of the piano—was first introduced in Boston in 1825. The modern piano was just being developed during Beethoven's last years. But his earliest sonatas had showed up the limitations of the old piano and proved the need for a richer and more powerful instrument.

Nanette Streicher, who had become an accomplished pianist, understood Beethoven's music and encouraged him. In the year that she found him with "not a shirt that was whole," she was forty-three.

In troublesome times the Streichers were a great comfort to Beethoven. Fully devoted, they were never offended by his eccentricities.

It was about this time—while Napoleon was invading Russia—that Beethoven struck up a friendship with a man who was a strange mixture of mechanic and scientist. His name was Mälzel. He was the inventor of a mechanical tempo-marking device which he was eager for Beethoven to see. His invention consisted of a little hammer which, through a cog wheel and weight, tapped on a little wooden anvil. This was the first model. Later Mälzel designed it as a spring-driven pendulum, the instrument we know today as the "metronome."

Beethoven approved of this device, which could indicate the composer's exact tempo. But Mälzel was a man of many facets. He had once constructed a mechanical chess player in which a man was concealed. He also designed a mechanical brass band, all enclosed in a single case, which he called the "Panharmonicon." A cylinder with pins, like that of a music box, controlled the mechanism. He had had some compositions set into cylinder pins and he was eager to have Beethoven write directly for his mechanical instrument.

In the meantime he experimented with hearing aids. He designed several types of tin horns for Beethoven to try.

Besides his mechanical ingenuity, Mälzel had good business sense. And since both he and Beethoven were very short of money, Mälzel suggested that they join forces and try to take advantage of the political situation in Europe.

In England the fever of jubilation was running high. The reason was Wellington's victory in Spain over the French armies, led by Napoleon's brother, Joseph Bonaparte. The Battle of Vittoria, together with the complete defeat of the French Army in Russia, were the first cracks in Napoleon's imperial wall.

All Europe was happy. But England, Napoleon's main enemy, was joyful. Mälzel, knowing that Beethoven was already something of a legend in England, was quick to grasp the oportunity. He therefore proposed that Beethoven write a battle piece celebrating Wellington's victory. This he wanted written for his mechanical music box, which he would then exhibit in England. With Beethoven's name, Wellington's victory and his own novel music machine all together, Mälzel was certain of success and money. Battle pieces were very popular. Mälzel was so enthusiastic that he even mapped out the musical sequences for Beethoven. These sequences, of course, included the national anthems of all the nations involved.

Oddly enough, because of the defeat of that betrayer of

his early hopes, Napoleon, or perhaps only because of what he called his "unbuttoned mood," Beethoven was agreeable to this unmusical adventure. He began to write for the gallery. He seemed happy about it and made an entry in his notebook, "It is certain that one writes very gratefully when one is writing for the public; also that one writes rapidly."

But before his notes could be hammered into cylinder pins, there was a change in plans. Since Austria had lost many soldiers in the battles against Napoleon, leaving many widows and children, Mälzel, organized a charity concert. For the benefit of the crowd, Beethoven's *Battle Symphony* would be played by a live orchestra. And for the benefit of musical Vienna the new *Seventh Symphony* by Beethoven would also be performed. This benefit for the soldiers' widows and children would be the first performance of both new works.

Famous musicians in Vienna fell in with the scheme and filled out the orchestra. Meyerbeer himself worked the important battle drums and the famous pianist Moscheles crashed the cymbals. Fun was had by all. The concert was such a great success that, by popular demand, it was repeated four days later. The *Battle Symphony* was a sensation. Beethoven had never had such acclaim. And charity gained 4,000 florins from the two performances.

On the wave of this success Beethoven now secured a concert hall and for his own benefit repeated the *Battle Symphony*, together with his *Seventh Symphony* and his new *Eighth Symphony*. This concert, like the others, was a great success.

The concerts proved an advantage to Beethoven in still another way. Out of patriotic feeling a large audience was attracted. This large audience, which had come solely to hear the descriptive *Battle Symphony*, was what is called today a "captive audience." They also heard two new Beethoven symphonies. Thus a new and wider audience was exposed to Beethoven's serious work. By hearing this new music they could learn to understand it and like it.

In all this Mälzel and his mechanical music box were left out. He still had hopes, however, of bringing Beethoven to London along with his music box, which would bang out Wellington's victory.

But now, with such success in Vienna, Beethoven did not see the need for going to England. As for the pins in the cylinders, Beethoven felt that the *Battle Symphony* could be better performed by an orchestra.

Mälzel was angry. He secretly obtained parts of the music score, hammered in the cylinder pins and, leaving Vienna, proceeded to give concerts. Now Beethoven was angry and instigated a lawsuit. Mälzel claimed that the symphony was written for his machine. The case hung in the law courts for several years. In the end the suit was dropped, each litigant agreeing to pay half the costs.

Besides attracting the attention of Europe to Beethoven, Mälzel accomplished something else that was good. Beethoven highly approved of the metronome and accordingly marked the tempo on all his compositions. Thus, because of Mälzel, we know today the exact tempo that Beethoven intended.

Beethoven, when he entered his suit against Mälzel, already had two lawsuits pending over his contract with Prince Kinsky and Prince Lobkowitz. The three cases were in the courts at the same time. The broil of contention is certainly not conducive to creative work. This perhaps is one reason why, during these years, Beethoven was not very productive. But there was still another and perhaps more important reason. Beethoven, as we shall soon see, was coming to the end of a period. It was a critical time. Emotionally it was just as disturbing as that other crisis in his life, the time when he wrote the strange Heiligenstadt document. The Heiligenstadt crisis ushered in that wonderful creative period which began with the *Eroica*. This coming crisis was also to mark the definite end of a time and the beginning of Beethoven's last and most wonderful creative period.

It was the great success of the *Battle Symphony* that prompted the revival of Beethoven's opera *Fidelio*. Ironical as it may seem, this *Battle Symphony*, a blasting piece of musical claptrap, was Beethoven's greatest success to date. On this success he was able to drag along other works, works of genuine worth, some even stamped with immortality.

No longer could he complain of Vienna and the stupidity of the unmusical public. Now he was truly successful and even famous.

The years 1813, 1814 and 1815, the worst years for Napoleon, were the best years for Beethoven. He was more careful with the money that came to him and he was able to save 8,000 florins, which he invested in bank shares.

Besides money, he was about to receive very special honors. With that spectacular adventurer Napoleon now defeated and exiled to the island of Elba, the rulers of Europe gathered for the Congress of Vienna.

The Czar Alexander, who took the credit for Napoleon's terrible defeat in Russia, was one of the great heroes of the day. His ambassador, Count Razoumowsky, for whom Beethoven wrote three of his most famous quartets, lost no time in presenting Beethoven to the dazzling rulers of Europe. The Archduke Rudolph, who was devoted to his old piano teacher, insisted that all foreign dignitaries coming to his palace should meet Beethoven.

When Beethoven bowed before the Empress of Russia, she was most complimentary and this pleased him so much that he was inspired to write a little polonaise for her. Very soon a special concert of Beethoven's music was given in the royal palace. In connection with this concert, Beethoven had a singular honor, one which probably no composer, before or since, has enjoyed. He was permitted to invite the sovereigns of Europe in his own name. And once more that bombastic *Battle Symphony* brought tremendous applause. Surprisingly enough, Beethoven's *Seventh Symphony,* played at the same concert, also received a share of commendation.

The concert was a great success and, as more and more distinguished visitors arrived in Vienna, it was repeated twice during the month of December 1814. Beethoven was in high spirits. In January there was still another concert, at the end of which Beethoven rose to acknowledge the applause. After bowing several times, he suddenly went to the piano, sank his head low and began to improvise before all present: emperors, kings, queens, princes, dukes, counts and ministers of state. He gave them something they had never before heard, something the world has never heard since.

This was the last time Beethoven ever appeared as a pianist in public.

Suddenly it all ended. Like a gust of wind that blows the autumn leaves, stripping bare the trees, the royal visitors fled from Vienna. They fled in terror. News had arrived that Napoleon had escaped from Elba and was marching with a fresh army toward Paris.

Vienna was soon empty. Beethoven's honors quickly faded and the applause became only the echo of a memory.

In November of this same year of 1815, Beethoven's brother Karl died. Karl, no doubt influenced by Beethoven himself, by his desperate loneliness and by his disregard for Karl's wife, had made a will appointing Beethoven guardian of his nine-year-old son. But the dying father of young Karl added the following paragraph to the will: "Inasmuch as the best harmony does not exist between my brother and my wife . . . I by no means desire that my son be taken away from his mother . . . the guardianship to be exercised by her as well as my brother. Only by unity can the object which I had in view in appointing my brother guardian of my son be attained. Wherefore, for the welfare of my child, I recommend compliance to my wife, and more moderation to my brother. God permit them to be harmonious for the sake of my child's welfare. This is the last wish of the dying husband and brother."

But alas! Beethoven could not comply with his brother's wishes. Eight days after the funeral, he filed a petition in court, asking for sole guardianship of young Karl on the grounds that the boy's mother was unreliable, had loose morals, and was guilty of infidelity. Perhaps some evidence may have been found against the woman for the court upheld the charges of Beethoven and gave him custody of the child. Beethoven, pleased at his victory, shook hands with everyone in the courtroom and swore that he would perform his duties.

Thus did Beethoven, his heart filled with good intentions,

take on an obligation which was to bring him a crushing weight of grief. The boy was nine years old; thirty-six years his junior. Temperamentally and by long habit Beethoven was the last man in the world to be a father. His life was not adjusted to include such a responsibility. Even his disorderly home was unfit for a child. Beethoven's moodiness, his deafness, his isolation and his irregular mode of living were all in the way.

The young Karl, separated from his mother whom he loved, was miserable. From the very first day of the guardianship to the very last day of Beethoven's life, Karl brought his distinguished uncle nothing but grief and misery.

It was not the fault of the boy. It was the fault of circumstances. It was the fault of pride, of aching loneliness, of an unfilled void, of intolerance. As in that disastrous family feud in Linz, Beethoven again displayed his complete lack of understanding of simple affairs of the world. This lack of understanding is part of Beethoven's character.

It was a strange time, a time of crisis for Beethoven. A time of brooding. A time for reflection.

For a number of years, since 1810, he had produced prolifically. The *Seventh* and *Eighth* symphonies were done quickly, in 1812, from notes which had been made some years before. They repeated an earlier manner and added only a little to round out that rich, dramatic and wonderfully emotional second period. But the little they added was important. Richard Wagner called the *Seventh Symphony:* "The dance in its highest condition, the happiest realization of the movements of the body in ideal form." All agree that the *Eighth Symphony* is inferior to the *Seventh*. Yet Hector Berlioz wrote that one of its movements "fell straight from heaven into the brain of its author, and was written down in one stroke." But with all this praise, these symphonies only embellished the wonderful second period without adding a new dimension.

Once the style of his middle period was established, Beethoven might have continued and produced more in like manner. But his spirit was too restless to mirror a mode and keep repeating. "His tumultuous vigor and full-voiced sentiment were too wild," says the music historian, Burk. "He could advance no further on the road of impulsive fervor, for he had passed his peak of hot-bloodedness. . . . Music had always come to his rescue. For once it seemed to fail him. Now he stood at a crossroad, impotent and confused, entirely without a sense of direction."

The experiences which had made up the substance of his creative work were not to be repeated. He was finished with walking that hard road, beset with its demons. He was done with its nobility and its pride. Even the final victory lost its brilliance and seemed nothing but tarnished tinsel.

Little by little Beethoven became the prisoner of his own solitude. Slowly he became aware that by a strange chain of circumstances he had been edged out of the ordinary family of mankind. Love, marriage, children, and the usual pleasures of a domestic home were denied to him. He carried within him a starved instinct of fatherhood. And because of this desperate need he clung to Karl, separated him from his mother and hoped that the boy would give him the missing warmth.

He was slowly becoming resigned to the bitterness of loneliness. Deprived of hearing the sound of his own music, he was gradually separating himself from the living world.

The silence was like a tomb; it was, in the words of Sullivan, "terrible and complete. But we may suppose that even then he was becoming aware that his separation from the world was the entry into a different and more exalted region."

Beethoven's love for his nephew was a blind reaching out to make one more attempt to find warm affection in the world of humans. Was the door closed against him? Where was love? Where was God? Can one go on and maintain hope and courage without love and without God?

Thus it was that a time had ended. A whole night of life had fallen about him. And the faint dawn that he felt might be coming could arrive only through spiritual reflection. His life was bound to the rock of music. Only music could deliver him.

During this dark period he was no longer eager to battle with Fate, for he writes in his notebook: "Fate, show your force! We are not lords over ourselves. What is determined must be, and so let it be!" And another entry reads, "Live in your art alone. Limited as you now are by your hearing, this is the only existence for you."

How different are these expressions from that cry of defiance, when he faced his oncoming deafness during the first crisis. It was then that he had called out, "No, I cannot endure it. I will take Fate by the throat. It shall not wholly overcome me."

So it was that a crisis again ushered in a new period in Beethoven's creative life. This time the battleground was not in the heart of Man.

In the third and final period we discover a music completely different from anything ever before created. Here we find a detachment from the mortal world and a deep spiritual reflection. In this, for a second time, he has given music a completely new dimension.

13

❧

KARL

THE STORY of Karl would be of little importance were it not bound so closely to those last agonizing years of Beethoven's life. For a hundred years music historians have blamed Karl for all the grief he brought to his uncle. There are some biographers who sincerely feel that Karl prevented Beethoven from composing masterpieces which the world has lost. It has been said that he was a miserable, wretched and worthless youth. That he was a gay blade, a rake. That he enjoyed cafés, billiards, balls and the society of gay ladies. That he was deceptive, untruthful and even committed petty larceny.

All of this can be found in the records. But in recent years, with more research and clearer vision, this evil view of Karl has undergone revision. Karl emerges now as an ordinary boy and not truly a bad boy. His behavior is typical of some boys who come from broken homes, boys who become problems in their new abode and enemies of society. Karl's home was broken by the death of his father and the separation from his mother. For this last act Beethoven was himself responsible. But if we understand his crying need at the time of crisis, we cannot be too harsh with him.

Beethoven was eager to train his nephew and have him become a musician, and if possible even a composer. But Karl had little talent for music and no desire to be a musician. This Beethoven refused to admit for a long time.

Since his home was in no condition to receive a child, Beethoven managed for two years to keep Karl in a fashionable boarding school. But this was expensive and at length he brought him home.

Resentful against his uncle and against society, Karl was so ill-mannered that it was necessary to engage a private tutor. At the same time Beethoven tried to influence the boy against his mother. Karl soon discovered that by shouting abuses against his mother into his deaf uncle's ear he could ingratiate himself. Because of this deafness it was not too often that Karl spoke to his uncle.

Here we come to another strange contradiction in the life of Beethoven. He loved Karl. He was certain he would turn out a genius. "You can propose a riddle in Greek to him," the proud uncle would say. He spent money on him and gave him money to spend. His whole life seemed to center on Karl. All this is true and still Karl was badly neglected. The home was a stable. He was filthy and dirty.

How is it that love, affection and devotion can lead to such miserable neglect!

The servants were sorry for Karl and from time to time they secretly allowed him to see his mother.

After about three years of this kind of existence, Karl at last ran away. He ran to his mother. Beethoven was disturbed.

He feared the woman would run off with Karl to Hungary or some other far-off place.

But the unfortunate mother again—for the third time—appealed to the court for justice. The case came up in the *Landrecht* court.

The testimony revealed that the mother, out of her meager income, was paying for half of the boy's support. Also that Beethoven at first allowed her only one brief visit a month to see her boy, and now did not allow her to see him at all. She had gone to the servants in the Beethoven home and from them she had learned that her son was being poisoned against her; that he was neglected, neither properly clothed nor washed. She had heard, also, that Beethoven intended sending him to a school, in a place far away. If he did so, she feared she would never see her son again.

It was also brought out in court that Karl was very lonely in his uncle's home; that he had no companions of his own age; and that at one moment he received affectionate coddling from his uncle who, in the next moment, would break out in a rage against him. The boy stole pennies to buy candy. He called the servants by insulting names. And although Beethoven forced him to kneel down twice a day in prayer, the result of all Beethoven's efforts at religious instruction was more harmful than beneficial. A priest in court testified that the uncle inspired the boy to speak against his mother and this was a sinful violation of one of the Ten Commandments.

The case would have gone on, but it was discovered that the *van* in Beethoven's name had no implication of nobility. It is not like the German *von*. Therefore the case was shifted from this court of "peers" to the lower court.

Beethoven tried to use his name and influence in the court.

He wrote a long and emotional letter to the judges, accusing the boy's mother and praising his own virtues. This long document closed with the following lines: "May it be clear from all this . . . that I may rightly be called his father! No motive, public or private, can be ascribed to me, other than the love of virtue; indeed the law courts themselves have admitted as much and thanked me for my parental care." He could not understand why he was not considered a good parent.

The result of this litigation was that the mother and a Viennese official were appointed legal guardians of the boy. Beethoven lost his case completely.

He was now in a most disturbed state. He engaged a distinguished lawyer and appealed the case to a higher court. This litigation lasted for months. The battle for Karl raged on and on. In the end Beethoven won. He was awarded guardianship, together with his friend Councilor Peters.

This Peters is not to be confused with Carl Peters, the music publisher to whom, at about the same time, Beethoven promised the manuscript of his *Missa Solemnis in D*. One of the great wonders of the world is that while the harrowing litigation over Karl was going on, month after month, Beethoven could keep on working on this new composition. This great Mass in D was Beethoven's tribute to his devoted patron Archduke Rudolph on his elevation to Archbishop. It was a moral debt which Beethoven hoped to repay in a sacred manner.

But how about his home, the home he promised to make for Karl? Here is a record of about that time, written by a friend. "It was four o'clock in the afternoon. As we entered we learned that in the morning both servants had gone away, and that there had been a quarrel after midnight which had disturbed all the neighbors . . . In the living room, behind a locked door, we heard the Master singing parts of the fugue of the Credo—singing, howling, stamping . . . The door opened and Beethoven stood before us with distorted features, calculated to incite fear. He looked as if he had been in mortal combat with the whole host of contrapuntists, his everlasting enemies. His first utterances were confused . . . Then he spoke of the day's happenings and with obvious restraint remarked, 'Pretty doings, these! Everybody has run away and I haven't had anything to eat since yesterday noon.' " The friends went out and came back with some food.

Beethoven never gave up the idea that Karl might turn out to be a genius. He had Czerny give him piano lessons, and now and then, because his deafness made conversation difficult, he wrote him letters containing moral precepts: "My dear son. . . . Rise early as various things may occur to you in the morning, which you could do for me. It cannot be otherwise than becoming in a youth, now in his nineteenth year, to combine his duties toward his benefactor and foster-father with those of his education and progress. I fulfilled my obligations toward my own parents."

There was never any real understanding between Beethoven and his nephew. In a letter to a friend Karl referred to his distinguished uncle as "the old fool."

Then suddenly in 1825, when Karl was nineteen, he announced that he had had enough of education and all those things like music, and would like to join a good army regiment.

There were many scenes. More lectures on morality. Beethoven tried to keep him at home at night, but, with one excuse or another, Karl managed to get out. He had his own friends now. They played billiards. Now and again he tried to make a little pocket money for himself by gambling. Beethoven sent friends out to spy on the youth and sometimes they found him in dance halls of ill repute. Such reports threw Beethoven into a state of panic.

This kind of existence continued for another year. At length Karl declared that he could endure it no longer. Beethoven was at his wits' end. Karl had told Schlemmer that he was capable of killing himself. Schlemmer reported this to Beethoven, together with the fact that he had discovered that Karl had a loaded pistol and that he had taken it away from him.

Then Karl ran away and Beethoven searched for him over a long week end, without success. He was worried.

It was learned later that Karl had gone to a pawnbroker, pledged his watch, and bought two pistols, which he loaded with powder and balls. He took a carriage to Baden and the next morning went to a place near some ruins, a place that had inspired Beethoven by its natural beauty. Here he raised the two loaded pistols to his temples and pulled both triggers.

A teamster driving by on this quiet Sunday morning saw his body, his hair and face covered with blood. The youth was still conscious. The teamster put him in his cart and drove him to Vienna and to his mother's home. Beethoven was informed of what had occurred. He rushed to Karl's bedside and sent for his friend, the surgeon Smetana.

When the blood was washed away and the wound examined, it was found that one pistol had missed completely and that the ball of the other pistol had merely grazed and lacerated the scalp and had not penetrated the skull.

Was Karl really such a bad shot? Or was this only the act of a tortured and unhappy youth, an act designed to bring attention to his misery and perhaps secure a more decent existence? These questions have puzzled some biographers.

To the police magistrate who questioned his intention Karl said that he did it because he was "tired of life" and because his uncle tormented him too much. Then he added, "I grew worse because my uncle wanted me to be better."

The case was now in the hands of the Viennese police. To complicate matters, Beethoven discovered that Karl had stolen some of his books and sold them. This act, he feared, if it came to the knowledge of the police, would brand his nephew as a felon. Karl might even have to spend time in prison.

Therefore Beethoven was ready to accept the idea that Karl should join a regiment. That would get him out of Vienna and away from the Viennese police until everything could be forgotten.

In this way did Beethoven's guardianship over his brother's son terminate. It was a dismal failure from beginning to end. And it lasted for twelve full years—until the very end of Beethoven's life. It persisted and endured, a wretched and perverse overtone, through Beethoven's entire last creative period.

But these were earthly troubles and hardly touched his new detached and reflective musical state. His difficulties with Karl may certainly have limited his creative production. They may even have hastened his death. But to the very end he remained devoted to Karl and he made him his sole heir. The passion for something domestic, for fatherhood, was strong in him.

14

JOURNEY INTO A NEW WORLD

THE SORDID adventure of Beethoven and his nephew Karl is now only a faded page of a history long past. Such domestic difficulties have happened in many families and in many lands.

The important thing is the music that was written during Beethoven's worrying years with Karl. The music is important, very important. For such music has not happened, before or since, in any land.

But the detachment and the journey into a new world did not come suddenly and at once. There was a joining link, a composition which presented both the "take Fate by the throat" defiance and the acquiescence and spiritual detachment of his last creative period. This joining link, a kind of progressive modulation, is presented in the *Hammerklavier Sonata*, No. 29 (Op. 106).

It was while working on this sonata in 1818 (and this is the year of his lawsuits against Karl's mother!) that Beethoven also projected two other great works, the *Missa Solemnis in D*

and the *Ninth Symphony* which had been commissioned by
the Philharmonic Society in London.

The *Missa Solemnis* he had hoped to have ready in two
years' time to perform at the ceremony when his patron
Archduke Rudolph was installed as the Archbishop of Ol-
mütz. But the work was protracted, and was not completed
until 1822. Its creation occupied Beethoven for a full four
years, and it was not published for another five years.

As for the *Ninth Symphony*, which is also known as
the *Choral Symphony*, this work had a strange evolution.
Snatches of melodies and motives for this symphony had
been running through Beethoven's head for thirty years. But
the parts were oddly separated and refused to fuse. In fact,
his sketchbook contains notes for two related symphonies, a
Ninth and a *Tenth*. Both were to employ singing voices. In
one, the text of a Greek myth dealing with the festival of
Bacchus was to be used. In contrast with this worship of the
pagan gods, the other symphony was to employ a sacred song
in praise of Jehovah. These dual religious forces had often
intrigued and occupied Beethoven's mind.

The sketchbooks show that in 1818 both related symphonies were in his mind. In time, in the high heat of his creative
furnace, they were fused together. Some pagan ideas were
thrown out completely and replaced by a long string of memories.

This *Ninth Symphony* was begun in 1818 to fulfill an agreement made with the Philharmonic Society the summer
before, through his old pupil Ries who was then living in
London. The Society offered Beethoven 300 guineas to come
to London the following year with two new symphonies, his
Ninth and *Tenth*.

But before he could settle down to these symphonies, he wanted to clear the deck of ideas that had accumulated and which he wanted to express in his *Hammerklavier Sonata.* And so the symphonies had to wait.

From its opening fortissimo chords, the *Hammerklavier Sonata* announces its violent and turbulent force. Until then the *Appassionata* had been outstanding in its overwhelming power and energy. But the *Hammerklavier,* in the opinion of Schauffler, "makes more strenuous demands upon the instrument, the performer, and the listener than any other composition of the Master." The wooden case that holds the piano's mechanism together seems ready to fly apart. And on the authority of Burk, here "was another sudden release of strength, goaded by duress of suffering."

While working on this composition Beethoven said to Czerny, "Just now I am writing a sonata which shall be my greatest." If it is not the greatest, it certainly is the longest, perhaps the longest ever written. It is as long as a full symphony. In the standard edition (edited by Artur Schnabel) the music runs to seventy-three pages.

The work cannot be dismissed because of length or because of the demands it makes on the performer, instrument, and listener. It must stand on its own merits, and these we must seek out. For the music of this last period, even the "modulating" link is important.

Its importance is clearly stated by Sullivan. "Beethoven's realization of his essential loneliness was terrible and complete. But we may suppose that even then he was becoming aware that his separation from the world was the entry into a different and more exalted region. But the *Hammerklavier*

Sonata is the expression of a man of infinite suffering, of infinite courage and will, but without God and without
hope. . . . The *Hammerklavier Sonata* does not belong to
what is called Beethoven's Third Period. Neither does it belong to the Second. It stands alone, a great and grim memorial to the long and painful journey between the two
worlds."

The energetic first movement is savage, stark and resolute.
Yet, although it displays courage, the demons on the road
seem to be missing. And the joy of conflict in which victory
is implied is certainly missing.

This first movement is followed by a *Scherzo*. It is pleasing
but it cannot be too joyful for it serves to introduce the
strange and most wonderful mood of the slow *Adagio*. Now
we seem to have set foot on that distant shore of a world
beyond.

Of this movement Bülow wrote, "The pain that tears the
heart no longer has the word here, but—as it were—tearless
resignation rigid as death." And Sullivan sees in this slow
movement "the deliberate expression, by a man who knows
no reserves, of the cold immeasurable woe in whose depths,
it would seem, nothing that we could call life could endure.
It seems as inimical to human existence as the icy heart of
some remote mountain lake."

Here again the accent is on death. And this slow movement, which plays for twenty minutes, is perhaps the longest
in all piano literature. Burk asks, "Who will explain all that
lay upon his spirit as he wrote the slow-moving chain of
heavy chords . . . ? It is inward, soul-searching music without
a doubt, its color sometimes dark and haunted . . . notes
climb to the highest register of the piano and give a strange

sense of dreaming upon a remote altitude. . . . Agitation can assault but no longer ravage his deep peacefulness."

These authorities attest to the sublime greatness of this music, to its remoteness and detachment. The far-off distant shore has been reached. The resignation has in it the peace and the cold beauty of death but it breathes softly with the warmth of life.

But on this note the sonata is unable to end. A final fugue, violent and stark, informs the listener that the furious struggle is not ended and that man must retain the will to resist his destruction, with blind energy and instinctive animal faith. The music in its fury tries to tear the piano apart.

Thus we see that surrender and acquiescence are not complete. The shore of ecstasy has been touched, as though in a dream, but now with the awakening there is a return to a former mortal experience.

Although the *Hammerklavier Sonata* gives us the first contact with that distant shore, the work has great difficulties. It is rarely played because of its demands on the performer and on the audience. Schauffler recalls that perhaps only once in his entire musical career has he heard it played successfully. He concludes by saying that, "During this life one does not expect to see the day when the *Hammerklavier* shall be adequately performed, on an adequate instrument, to adequate listeners." But he suggests that perhaps we will hear it well rendered in the world beyond.

And now we ask: Was it necessary to make it so long, so difficult, so impossible, that even after a century and a half no virtuoso has successfully rendered its full spirit and substance? Why?

The answer is simple. Beethoven's technique had grown

steadily. His art, his musical development had leaped forward. He himself was not bothered with the difficult piano technique. And the length was necessary for what he needed to say. These were considerations outside the realm of creative art and the expression of Beethoven's compulsive emotional experience.

Beethoven was not a writer of church music, nor did he have much feeling for the voice. When he wrote vocal music he made it almost impossible for the singer and when some complained he said, "Singers should be able to do anything except bite their own noses!" He seemed to take pleasure in making things difficult for the shrill sopranos. In the *Choral Symphony* it is almost impossible for the sopranos to get through their intricate shrieking noises. He has been charged with being a "tyrant over all vocal organs." From all this, one could almost conclude that he did not hold singing or singers in high regard. The music that ran through his head, he once said, always sounded as if it came from "some instrument."

Launched on the *Mass*, because of his wish to do homage to his patron, he at once ran into difficulties with the text. Since he knew little Latin he had the words translated into German. But the German words could not fit the rhythms and accents of the Latin. The next difficulty was one of simple belief. Beethoven's was a religion all its own. It consisted of a strange mixture of Eastern, Western, pagan, and personal credo that joined the beauty of nature with the inner strength of man.

Here at once there was a conflict. Schauffler believes that certainly "There were even affirmations in the *Credo* which he must have actively disbelieved. So it is hard to see how he could have entered in the composition of the *Missa* with that whole-hearted, enthusiastic conviction which is a necessary antecedent for the greatest works of art."

But Beethoven's mystical outlook could accept this theological skeleton and clothe it with a vast variety of ideas, all drawn from his inner storehouse in which Christian, pagan and Oriental experiences were bound together by Strength and the heroic in man. And this sacred storehouse was guarded by the Supreme Being himself.

Thus the form, or skeleton, on which he built the living tissue presented some difficulty. But he was master of all difficulties. In fact, the difficulties only seemed to help him, for in surmounting them, he brought his music out of the ordinary and onto a higher plane.

He gave little attention to traditional church service and followed the path he knew. He built his *Mass* as though it were a symphony to which he added the necessary words. To its outer form he gave an ecclesiastical robe. That is why some critics have called it a "sacred symphony with solo and chorus." This sacred symphony forms an appropriate link between his *Eighth* and the final *Ninth*.

On the first page of the score he wrote, "From the heart, may it speak to the heart." He was aware that his music was difficult to understand and perhaps not in the popular manner. He was also aware of his own difficulties with this form.

Some critics have felt that parts of the *Mass* are weak and confused and that the words often get in the way of the music and the dramatic treatment. Some even say that it stands below Bach, below Handel and even below Beethoven's own best compositions.

But all agree that here we are in the presence of something

magical and wonderful, something profound and beyond ordinary spiritual experience. The French composer Vincent d'Indy sums up Beethoven's *Mass* in a single line: "We stand in the presence of one of the greatest masterworks in the realm of music."

Out of a troubled time and confronted with a hundred difficulties, Beethoven emerged with a great masterpiece. Now he fully touched that mystical, far-off, detached and profound other shore. The shore of a new world.

The *Mass* was not finished until 1822. Beethoven was eager to have it published and he hoped he could publish it himself by raising subscriptions from the royal courts of Europe.

He wrote to Goethe to find out if the court of Weimer might possibly desire copies of the *Mass*, which would not be published in the ordinary way. But alas! Goethe never replied. Any more than he replied to Schubert who, in sending him the manuscript of his *Erlkönig*, asked for permission to dedicate this music to him.

In the end Beethoven managed to raise ten subscriptions at 50 ducats each—about $120—for the publication of his *Mass*. The royal subscribers were the courts of Russia, France, Denmark, Prussia, Saxony, the duchies of Tuscany and Hesse-Darmstadt, Prince Galitzin and Prince Radziwill of Russia and the Cecilia Society at Frankfurt.

With the *Mass* completed, Beethoven plunged into his *Choral Symphony*, which, as we have seen, had originally been conceived as two symphonies. Both had been promised to the London Philharmonic. Now the symphony began to take form but not without its inner problems.

The main subject took on gigantic proportions. Here were

gods themselves wrestling for the soul of man. This encounter seems to take place under a vast starless dome, where in half-light and half-mist, the sorrow of man is weighed against the world itself.

The first three movements are acknowledged universally to be of the highest musical magnitude. They are as noble as the best sections of the *Eroica* and of the *Mass*. Together, these three movements represent Beethoven's most original contribution to music.

But now we come to that last, and choral, movement. About this much has been written. There are some biographers, like Marion Scott, who see nothing incongruous in concluding a spiritual work with Schiller's drinking song, "The Ode to Joy." "Nor did he feel anything irreverent about it," says Scott, "since the symbolism of the True Vine runs all through the Christian religion."

But Sullivan, who has made a deep study of Beethoven's spiritual development, is disappointed at this concluding movement. He writes, "We feel that the spirit which has climbed up the heights of those three movements should now, like Moses on Sinai, be granted a vision of God Himself." But instead we are returned to a mortal world with a rejoicing that is completely devoid of sublime ecstasy. The very sound of the voice is itself a return to the mortal. "That Beethoven himself felt this inadequacy," Sullivan adds, "is nearly certain from the evidence we have."

Beethoven had great difficulty in introducing this movement with its voices after the first three movements. But he accomplished it in a masterful manner. After sounding the theme in simple quiet unison he develops some passages partly noisy and partly dissonant. Thus he introduces the

timbre of the human voice. Now it is natural for the baritone
to enter with this recitative, "Oh, friends, no more these
sounds continue! Let us now raise our voices to a song of
sympathy, of gladness. O joy, let us praise thee!"

Of Schiller's "Ode to Joy," Beethoven only used part, less
than half. He had to reject many verses and lines because
they either lacked dignity or were not in keeping with the
whole. Some lines like "May the foam to Heaven go spurting!
Lift this glass to the Good Spirit," were just too cheap to use.

On the authority of Czerny we are told that, after the first
performance, Beethoven emphatically declared that he was
not pleased with the Hymn to Joy and desired to write a fresh
fourth movement, one without voices. Since he was now
totally deaf, he could not hear the performance, but somehow or other he felt it and was able to follow along. And he
considered this last movement a failure.

Many critics agree that Schiller's "Ode to Joy" pulls the
wonderful music down from its spiritual heights. The warm
beating heart liberated from all mortal coils is suddenly
clutched by an icy mortal hand, and this in the name of
pagan joy!

But in conclusion a good word may be said. Perhaps the
promise of the first three movements was more than he could
possibly deliver. He had climbed Sinai but the face of the
Lord could not be seen. And so he joined again the family
of men.

"This is the last occasion," Sullivan concludes, "in which
Beethoven addresses his fellow men as one of them. Hence-
forth he voyaged 'in strange seas of thought alone.'"

A little postscript must be added to complete the history
of this famous *Ninth Symphony*. At the opening concert in

Vienna, in the presence of the imperial family, Beethoven received a tremendous ovation. In fact, the applause was much greater than that received by the imperial family when they entered the hall. At this greater applause the Commissioner of Police rose and shouted, "Silence!" In imperial Austria such conduct was close to treason.

Also, it must be added that the concert in Vienna was in violation of the contract Beethoven had made with the London Philharmonic Society, who had commissioned the symphony and paid a sum of £50. The original agreement for two symphonies and personal appearance had been altered. For the sum of £50 the Society was to have exclusive performance rights for a year and a half, after which all rights would revert to the composer. Beethoven not only broke faith with the London Society but, without intention, added insult by dedicating his symphony to the King of Prussia.

The King of Prussia was pleased to have the work dedicated to him and to show his appreciation His Majesty presented Beethoven with a diamond ring. But the "diamond" was only glass!

Before turning to Beethoven's last five quartets, which occupied the few remaining years of his life and which reached the rarest of all musical atmospheres, a word or two should be said of the last three piano sonatas. These were the three which followed the transition sonata, the *Hammerklavier*, and concluded the immortal series of thirty-two.

These volumes of thirty-two sonatas present the most monumental work in all piano literature. There are some who, when shipwrecked on a desert island, would desire a Bible and a copy of Shakespeare. But others certainly would be more content with a piano and the thirty-two sonatas. With such a choice, it is hard to say who in isolation could get closer to a spiritual life.

The last three sonatas are very unlike the *Hammerklavier*. They are warm and intimate and seem to present a quartet quality of voices. They are free—free in idea and free in form. They break with the strict conventional sonata form and are almost close to imaginative fantasies. Now Beethoven seems content with a two-movement plan. He breaks another precedent by ending with a final slow movement. In spirit this is contrary to the hero impulse and the victory ending of his former works.

The last sonata, No. 32, seems to sum up all. The first movement has been called one of the most amazing and powerful melodies in all music. The second movement, built on a theme as simple as a folk song, moves on with its variations into sublime visions. The end is soft, melodic and quiet. Beethoven's friend Schindler thought that perhaps he had intended to add another movement, one that was swift, climaxed with a dance! But no, this was the end; an end in peace and quiet, far removed from the turmoil of mortal existence.

It was a quiet and affectionate farewell to the piano.

The piano and the orchestra were put aside. For thirteen years Beethoven had neglected the quartet and now he seemed to feel that what he desired to say could best be expressed with a chamber ensemble. He had completely outlived those noble, tuneful quartet discourses, designed for parlor entertainment.

Now it happened that Prince Galitzin, a wealthy Russian

amateur and patron of music, came to Vienna on a visit in 1822. This is the same Prince Galitzin who, in the following year, subscribed 50 ducats toward the publication of Beethoven's *Mass*.

Returning to his home in St. Petersburg he was filled with enthusiasm for a light operetta which Weber had written. He considered buying a copy of the score for his own use. However, the viola player of his private quartet, whose name was Zeuner, suggested that the money might be better spent if the prince would commission Beethoven to compose some new quartets. The light Weber operetta and Beethoven's quartets stood at opposite musical poles. But the prince thought it over and agreed that this was the better idea.

Since he was already thinking of writing chamber music, Beethoven accepted the proposal to compose three new quartets for Prince Galitzin, for which he was to be paid 50 ducats each (about $125).

Here is another name, Prince Galitzin, engraved on the pages of musical history through Beethoven. The name Galitzin would long ago have crumbled to dust were it not for his subscription toward the *Mass* and these three quartets.

Due to this rich Prince, the *Mass* received its first performance in St. Petersburg in 1824. And in this year Prince Galitzin had vision enough to write a most prophetic letter to Beethoven. "Your genius is centuries in advance and at the present time there is scarcely one hearer who is sufficiently enlightened to enjoy the full beauty of your music." These words were written even before the Prince received the first new quartet.

All this is to the glory of the name Galitzin. But on the dark page of his ledger there is a serious charge. He paid for the first quartet but not for the other two. Perhaps the music did not please him, or perhaps there was another reason. At any rate, it was long after Beethoven's death that the prince finally agreed to pay Beethoven's heir, Karl, the balance of the money due.

These are all trifling incidents. It is the music that is important. The events could easily be forgotten but the music remains. It fills a place that it has held for a century and a half, detached from the world and even from all other music. It stands alone.

After fulfilling his obligation to the prince and delivering the promised three quartets, numbered 12 to 14, Beethoven had by no means said all he had in mind. Driven on by the heat of creation, he went on writing and soon completed two more, which are numbered 15 and 16. These last five quartets, Nos. 12 to 16, are charged with Beethoven's greatest music, a music completely different from anything written before or since.

In these last quartets, especially the middle three, sometimes called "the A B C quartets," because their keys are A minor, B flat major and C sharp minor, we find that Beethoven has discovered a new region of consciousness. We are aware of strange seas, strange shores and chains of strange hills. We have touched a land that is new to us and yet this land is in a way strangely familiar. What is revealed is new. And yet it seems that we have always known it for it was ever with us, perhaps for a thousand years or more, and all this time it was locked away at the end of a long dark corridor of our subconscious.

How strange it is that sounds, scraped on the taut guts of

four stringed instruments, should have the power to liberate this thing long imprisoned within us. And now that it is free we ask: How is it that this wonderful revelation has for so long been kept in darkness, kept from us? Why has this thing, a thing beyond joy or sorrow, been hidden? Is it because we are poor underlings, little aware of even ourselves and not worthy of revelations that stem from within? Burk points out that there was a steady consistency to Beethoven's development. And he found its "utmost fulfillment in the last quartets."

A strange legend has grown up about Beethoven. It has been assumed that because he was poor and ill, and because of his deafness, he became an embittered recluse. That he was without friends and abandoned by the one creature he loved so desperately. That because of all these circumstances he turned to that "inner music" which led to the last quartets. This is sheer nonsense.

The last quartets contain no "inner music," any more than does the *Ninth Symphony*. In this music there is no withdrawal from the world and it certainly is not the product of a recluse. The legend is wrong. The picture is true but the conclusion false.

Beethoven's art was bound to the world we live in, the world of nature, of beauty, of warm-hearted people. His vision may have grown keener through his loneliness and his habit of brooding. But that vision, even though he voyaged alone "in strange seas of thought," always embraced a humanity that was free.

In his loneliness he found contentment. "When I am alone," he said, "I am never alone." His memories and his visions were wonderful companions and he was often their willing prisoner. That is how he fell into those *raptus* and that is how he became possessed.

Some creations are born and soon die. And some are born and live on and on. Life seems to stem from the creator who is possessed.

The first of the two quartets that Beethoven composed after completing the three for Prince Galitzin, was No. 14, in C sharp minor, Op. 131. It is this quartet that Beethoven himself felt was his greatest. And one of the last he wrote, No. 15, in A minor, Op. 132, is his next greatest. This opinion is not shared by all music critics, for some are inclined to give second place to the E flat major, No. 12, Op. 127, or even to another favorite. But most critics share Beethoven's high regard for the quartet in C sharp minor.

From Beethoven's notebooks we learn that this quartet portrays a single day in his life. Into this day he has poured a long stream of experiences, a flow of consciousness distilled by contemplated thought. These experiences run through seven movements. Breaking completely with classical form, the first movement is a slow fugue, reflective and serious. Richard Wagner has called this movement "perhaps the most heavy-hearted thing that has ever been expressed in tones." In fact, the entire quartet served Wagner as a liberating inspiration for his great operas.

The last piano sonatas—from the *Hammerklavier* on—and the fine, last quartets—considered as an entity—are spoken in a language that is spiritually charged. "Gone is the pathos of the earlier works," writes Alfred Einstein, "it lies far behind us. . . . In these sublime soliloquies of a lonely soul, ranging immeasurably beyond the confines of his age, the subject-matter tends to become simpler and more aphoristic, but the treatment and articulation ever subtler. . . . For us they represent in energy of form and spirituality, of content, the supremest height which music has attained."

In these last words, articulated in sound, Beethoven has described that aspiration of man that is bound to the prophetic dream.

It must not be assumed, because these last works are so wonderful and so highly praised by the best music authorities, that they are easily understood. For many years they have been neglected; only in recent times have they received general acceptance. Even today they are rarely performed. Many musicians have confessed that it has taken them years to know and appreciate these later works. Yet in the end they have found the experience most rewarding.

Secret things, long locked away and suddenly brought out into light, are not easily recognized. And when the vision is built of a prophetic dream substance, the difficulty is compounded.

That a high spiritual content in art may console and help man to take his place in humanity has long been known. This is so pronounced in Beethoven that many biographers have assumed that it must stem from one devoutly religious in the strict church sense. Vincent d'Indy is one who believed Beethoven "in his life and in his works, a believer." His love of nature, d'Indy feels, is the love of God in nature. And his deep sincerity in his *Mass* could come only from one who was reverent and piously devout. Is it possible that such deep sincerity could exist in art without having its origin in religion?

What is the actual evidence? What was the religion of Beethoven and how did this enter into his music?

First of all, Beethoven was born a Catholic, was baptized in the Church, and died a Catholic. But though he consented to receive the last rites of the Church, he always held himself aloof from organized religion. He visited nature but never the Church. His deep love of Greek and Roman mythology brought him intimately into Olympus. Here were gods who had human failings, gods he could easily understand. Often in his letters he mentioned the names of pagan gods. And often when he spoke of God, one did not know if he meant Jehovah or one of the Greek deities. To a friend who submitted a music manuscript to him on which was written, "By the help of God," Beethoven returned it with the words, "Better you help yourself."

During his last years he dipped into some of the sacred writings of the East. From an essay written by Schiller dealing with the religion of ancient Egypt, he copied some lines and he had the page framed and put under glass on his writing table. These lines served as his creed:

I am that which is.
I am all, what is, what was, what will be.
No mortal man has lifted my veil.
He is only and solely of himself and to him alone do all things owe their existence.

These words, always before him as he was writing, served to inspire him, to remind him that his creative power was within himself.

He also copied out a page from another Oriental religious

156]   BEETHOVEN AND THE WORLD OF MUSIC

work. This contains a long paragraph praising the Supreme Being Brahma, and concludes with the following lines, "Thou alone art the true, Blessed. Thou, the best of all laws, the image of all wisdom, present throughout the entire world. Thou attainest all things. Sun, Ether, Brahma." But Beethoven crossed out the last three words. There was probably something about them that he disliked.

And on the same page he copied a hymn which begins with the words, "Spirit of spirits, who spreading thyself through space and endless time art raised high over everything."

Strangely enough, these were ideas which fitted in with his mysticism. There is no record of his ever having copied out a section of the Bible. He knew some of the familiar Bible quotations, but he used them rarely.

Somehow or other, the spiritual values that he sought were those that did not conflict with his inner convictions. His early philosophy was founded on strength. And through strength he hoped to achieve. Strength to him meant industry and artistic integrity. Sweetness and light, meekness and that nonresistance that turns the other cheek were not in his philosophy.

He was in sympathy with pagan and Eastern gods for he felt in them a morality of the heart and other sympathetic aspects. He understood gods who had special tasks to perform, as Bacchus who was in charge of fertility, springtime, wine and the joy of living; or Minerva, who was worshiped as the goddess of wisdom. Still, he did not exclude Jehovah. He appealed to him in such lines as "may God give me strength" and he also, as we have seen, "cursed him for exposing his creatures to chance." He seemed to have all the gods of creation wrapped together in one concept.

When Beethoven says, "I know very well God is nearer to me than to other artists. I associate with Him without fear," we are not too certain of his choice of deity. Yet we understand that he is speaking of the Creator of all nature. His love of nature has brought him close to nature, closer than it has brought other artists. Therefore, his meaning is clear. The creator of Nature is his Supreme Being.

A knowledge of his spiritual values and his inner convictions would help us to understand the philosophical frame on which his music was built. The ideas of strength and hero are related. Together they struggle for freedom. Man is important. Victory and joy are also together. The rejected soul, sunk in sorrow and even despair, is raised out of its darkness, bathed in light and made part of all mankind.

Beethoven felt that all men were capable of nobility and that nobility of head and heart equaled the nobility of birth.

That is why he had so much difficulty finding a libretto for an opera. He needed the stuff out of which heroes were made. Besides *Egmont* nothing that Goethe wrote fitted in with Beethoven's inner convictions. Not even *Faust*. He did write a line or two in one of his notebooks, inspired by a few phrases from this long poetic drama. But the whole idea of *Faust* with its confused morality was foreign to him. This story, which involves the power of the devil, murder and infanticide, is not the material that Beethoven wove into the fabric of his music.

Macbeth appears as an idea in his notebook, but this tragedy is also very far removed from the spirit and substance of Beethoven's music. It is far from his spiritual ideas and in direct conflict with his beliefs.

Beethoven's strange and bold composite religion could not have embraced either subject. He had a religion of his own which he had designed for his own need. It is within these spiritual values that he is able to express those things which deeply concern mankind.

15

LAST DAYS AND LAST WORDS

IT WILL remain one of the wonders of this world that the great music of Beethoven's third period could have been written at a time when he was ill, alone, stone-deaf, harried by lawsuits, and forsaken by the one creature he loved.

When Karl's attempt at suicide and Beethoven's failure as a suitable guardian had been brought out in open court, both felt the sting of disgrace. Then it seemed necessary that Beethoven find a place where Karl could go for a few weeks. This would give his scalp wound a chance to heal before he presented himself to the army. It would also get Karl away from Vienna and a possible fresh arrest for having stolen and sold some books belonging to his uncle. Beethoven was not too well. The whole business had been such a shock that his friend Schindler thought "he looked like a broken old man of seventy."

Under these painful circumstances Beethoven accepted an invitation to visit his brother Johann and see his new 400-acre country estate on the banks of the Danube. The drug business had prospered. Johann was now a proud landowner.

Beethoven had avoided this summer estate because of his brother's wife, Therese. She was the woman he had once asked the police to escort from the town of Linz. She was still his enemy. And because he considered her of that "tribe" of evil women he had refused to come under her roof as a guest. But now there was the press of necessity. With protests and on condition that the woman remain in the background—as though she were still the housekeeper—he finally consented.

Johann came to Vienna in his carriage and called for Beethoven and Karl. The journey took two days. They rode in silence. Karl, with his bandaged head, sulked in his corner. Beethoven did not speak to his brother, partly because of his deafness and partly because he despised him and had nothing to say. Johann and Karl did not speak because they knew that Beethoven, being deaf, would be suspicious and would want them to write out their remarks in his conversation notebook. Besides, all this, Johann was angry. To him, his brother and nephew were meddlesome troublemakers.

In this way, with hatred and silence, the carriage brought them to the little town of Gneizendorf, where Johann had his fine estate. Beethoven was happy to be given a large room with a full view of the Danube. This stream of liquid history winding through the valley reminded him pleasantly of the river Rhine and his childhood.

During the days Beethoven remained in his room composing the last of his final quartets. Therese kept discreetly out of the way. Johann played the lord of the manor and impressed his nephew by driving about the estate in his carriage and showing how his tenants bowed and scraped before him.

Karl seemed most obliging and offered to go to town every day and bring back whatever was required. But soon he remained in town many hours, for he had found soldier friends, drinking companions, and a billiard hall. When Beethoven learned of this, he forbade Karl to leave the house. This loss of freedom Karl resented. Beethoven wanted desperately to win his nephew's affection but he did not know how. When he asked him why he sulked and was silent, Karl wrote in the conversation book, "You ask me why I am silent. Because I have had enough. I must endure everything."

A few weeks went by and the bandages were removed from Karl's head. Then a month went by and another half a month. Karl was now getting used to the easy country life and did everything possible to avoid returning to Vienna. He could get Beethoven to do anything he desired merely by pretending a little affection.

But at last the weather grew cold. Beethoven was not too well; his liver was making him uncomfortable. The summer house was not designed for winter living.

And so on the first of December, in a hired open cart which Beethoven later described to his doctor as "the devil's most wretched vehicle, a milk wagon," they started out for Vienna. They stopped for the night at an inn where Beethoven was forced to sleep in an unheated room. A fever and chill set in.

In the morning he was weak and still feverish. Karl helped him back into the open cart. The winter weather was hard upon them and they did not reach home until late evening. Beethoven went to bed with a fever and chills.

He had hoped that his strong physique would throw off this cold, but after two days with no relief, he finally sent for a doctor, who found symptoms of inflammation of the lungs. These symptoms were complicated by the condition of his liver, which puzzled the doctor.

A day or so later he began spitting blood and breathing

with difficulty. Pneumonia had set in. But this his doctor was able to relieve and in a few days he was able to sit up in bed. On the seventh day he was well enough to get out of bed and write some letters.

But as his lungs grew stronger, his liver and stomach brought him violent pains. Jaundice set in and dropsy brought on a general swelling. A surgeon was sent for and it was decided that the water should be drawn off. This was done; five and a half measures were taken, and the patient was greatly relieved. This was the first of a number of tappings. The date was December 20, 1826. For a time he was fairly comfortable. He was even in a mood to read.

As a convalescent Beethoven enjoyed a number of experiences. Gerhard, the thirteen-year-old son of Beethoven's old friend, Stephan von Breuning, to whom he had dedicated his violin concerto, came in after school. Beethoven loved Gerhard. He called him "Trouser Button."

Gerhard had affection for Beethoven, and in his childish hand wrote many lines in his conversation books, lines both simple and revealing. Here are some of them: "Has your belly grown smaller?" "You should perspire more." "Is the operation painful?"

Then the thirteen-year-old boy would open his book of classical history and together they would look at the pictures of the wonderful men and women who lived on Olympus.

When they were finished looking at pictures, Trouser Button would give Beethoven a lesson in arithmetic. The examples of simple division and multiplication are to be seen today in the conversation books.

Besides Trouser Button, there were other little pleasures. Beethoven read some of the novels of Sir Walter Scott and

Ovid's *Metamorphoses*, which of course tells of the wonderful adventures of the Greek gods.

Then one day, the musician Johann Stumpff sent Beethoven from London a set of forty volumes of the works of Handel. This was a wonderful present.

Young Gerhard tells of this in his recollections. "When I entered his room at noon as usual, he at once pointed out these works, piled up on the piano, while his eyes glowed with joy. 'Look, these were given to me today. These works have given me great pleasure. For a long time I've been wishing to have them; for Handel is the greatest, the most capable of composers; there is still much to be learned from him. Just hand me those books again!' "

To Stumpff in London Beethoven wrote, "Most worthy friend, my pen cannot describe the pleasure that you have given me by sending the works of Handel, by going so far as to make me a present of them (truly a royal present for me!). It has even been put in the newspaper here, and I enclose the cutting. Unhappily, for the last three months and until now I have been down with dropsy. . . . Physician, surgeon, chemist, everything must be paid. I remember quite well several years ago the Philharmonic Society wished to give a concert for my benefit. It would be a great good fortune for me if they could renew this intention: I might be saved, after all, from all the embarrassments that await me." The letter closed with the words, "Once more I appeal to your philanthropic heart in view of my position . . . and wishing you all that is fine and good, I send you my best regards."

Besides the music of Handel, Beethoven, while in bed, was able to see a large collection of Schubert's songs for the first time. His friend Schindler records the event in these words: "I submitted to him a collection of Schubert's songs and ballads, about sixty in number, and among them many that were still in manuscript at the time. I did so with the intention not only of providing him with an agreeable diversion, but also of giving him a chance to acquaint himself with the character of Schubert's work and talent. . . . The great Master, who previously had not known five songs by Schubert, was amazed by the number now shown him and would not believe that up to that time Schubert had already composed more than five hundred songs. . . . Repeatedly he exclaimed, full of happy enthusiasm, 'Truly, this Schubert is lit by a divine spark.' "

Schubert was then thirty years old. Although both composers lived in Vienna, they knew each other only slightly. Schubert was painfully shy. Now, with this appreciation and admiration, they might have become good friends. But alas! It was too late.

One day, Diabelli, the music publisher, brought Beethoven a present of a small engraving of the house in which Haydn was born. Beethoven was pleased with this gift and showed it to his friends. To Hummel he said, "Look, dear Hummel, the house where Haydn was born. It was given to me and it gives me great pleasure. Truly it is a wretched hovel in which so great a man was born!"

At last, on January 2, 1827, after many delays, Karl left to join the army. He and Beethoven quarreled the night before he left, and this aggravation did not help Beethoven's condition. A second tapping was necessary. Beethoven began to lose faith in his doctor, who was an amateur musician and also a tedious bore. He admired Beethoven and spoke to him about music. But Beethoven did not care to have a doctor's opinion about music. He wanted to be cured and return to his work.

In the first month of his illness it is recorded that the doctor prescribed, besides numerous powders and other medicines, seventy-five bottles of physic! Not only could this kind of medical treatment weaken a patient, but could even destroy him.

About the middle of January, Schindler and other friends finally succeeded in calling in Dr. Malfatti. Beethoven had once been his patient, but they had quarreled. Perhaps because Malfatti knew that Beethoven was a difficult person, he at first refused to come. This was the doctor who later, to protect his distinguished patient, destroyed all the medical records on Beethoven. But at last he consented to come.

Now everything seemed forgiven. Even Johann's wife Therese, whom Beethoven had long despised, was tolerated. She seemed to bear no great resentment, for she came to the house almost daily to take care of the sick man.

The condition of the house was not good. The invalid's bed was filthy. It was riddled by bedbugs. Stephan von Breuning and his wife, parents of Trouser Button, had the good sense to bring some insecticide. This probably helped a little. But the sick man was tortured all night long by the bugs. These unsanitary conditions were in keeping with the medical ignorance of the day. It was no worse in Vienna than in London or Paris or any other part of Europe at that time.

At first the change of doctors seemed to do some good. But then Beethoven grew worse and the old doctor—"that ass!" as Beethoven called him—was brought back.

B E E T H O V E N   A N D   T H E   W O R L D   O F   M U S I C

The days wore on with tiresome weariness. Early in March Beethoven wrote to his friends, the friend, the famous pianist, Moscheles, "On February 28, I was operated on for the fourth time and now there are signs that a fifth may be necessary. Where does all this lead to and what is to become of me if things continue in this way? Truly, a very hard lot has fallen to me! Yet, I am resigned to what Fate has ordained."

Alas! The Beethoven, with fire enough in his blood to set the world aflame, the Beethoven who once cried out, "I will take Fate by the throat. It shall not wholly overcome me," this Beethoven was now reduced, humbled and even resigned!

A few days after writing Moscheles, Beethoven received the good news that the London Philharmonic Society had "resolved to express their good will and lively sympathy" by sending Beethoven £100 sterling "to provide the necessary comforts and conveniences" imposed by the illness. Beethoven was overjoyed. Many times during the day he exclaimed, "May God reward them a thousandfold!"

He again wrote to Moscheles, asking him to "convey to the Philharmonic Society my heartfelt gratitude." He asked Moscheles to urge the Philharmonic Society not to abandon the idea of giving a charity concert from which they should deduct this gift of £100, and should the Society "be kind enough to remit the remainder to me, I guarantee to show the Society my most cordial gratitude by agreeing to write for them a new symphony, a sketch of which is already lying in my desk, or a new overture or anything else the Society may desire. And if heaven will only restore my health to me I will

show the generous English how well I appreciate their regard
for my unfortunate condition."

His close friends Schindler and von Breuning did not think
he should accept this money from London while he still had
bank shares valued at over 7,000 florins. His plea of poverty,
they thought, could not be supported by facts and the whole
affair would look ugly if the truth were known. But Beethoven brushed all these reasons aside by insisting that the
bank shares were already willed to Karl, and that by right he
was entitled to this little inheritance and therefore the bank
shares belonged to him and could not be touched.

The banker who came to deliver the funds from London
recorded, "I found Beethoven in a sad way, more like a skeleton than a living being. . . . He said quite openly that he
considered this money as a relief sent from heaven." The
banker proposed that he give him half the amount immedi-
ately and the other half later. But Beethoven replied that
half would not suffice for his present wants. "I therefore gave
him, according to his wish, the whole sum at once."

Toward the end of March, Schindler wrote to Moscheles that
Beethoven was at work on a quintet for strings, two movements being already finished and that he was also working on
"the *Tenth Symphony,* which he mentioned in his letter to
you." But alas! "He feels that his end is near, for yesterday
he said to me and von Breuning, 'Applaud, my friends. The
comedy is finished!'"

His friend, the piano virtuoso Hummel, had traveled across
Germany to be with Beethoven. He visited him almost daily,
bringing his wife with him. They sat by the bed and tried to
comfort Beethoven as he lay weak and miserable. He was

silent. Beads of perspiration stood out on his forehead. Hummel's wife took her handkerchief and dried his brow and face several times. He remained silent but looked up at her with a glance of gratitude.

On the twenty-third of March Beethoven signed a short will leaving all his possessions and all rights to his works to his nephew Karl. The next morning he gave permission for a priest to come and administer the last sacrament.

For two days more the strong man lay almost completely unconscious, breathing heavily and struggling to hold on to life. His friends gathered. They sat in the room. They waited. And then they departed and came again.

On the afternoon of March 26 a number of friends were at his bedside. Schindler and von Breuning left the house and walked over to the cemetery; they knew the end was near and the choice of a grave would fall to them. Several others also left the house.

Only a casual acquaintance, Hüttenbrenner, and Therese van Beethoven, remained and were present at the end. Hüttenbrenner later described the scene in these words: "After Beethoven had been unconscious, with the death rattle in his throat, from three o'clock in the afternoon until five, there suddenly came a flash of lightning, together with a violent clap of thunder, the glare of which lit up the death chamber. . . . Beethoven opened his eyes, lifted his right hand and looked up for several seconds, his fist clenched and a very serious, threatening expression on his face. . . . When he let his raised arm sink to the bed, his eyes closed halfway. . . . not another breath. Not a heartbeat more!"

This was the end. The clap of thunder sounded the final

chord. Beethoven was no more. His fifty-seven years of life were ended. The year was 1827.

The next day the loyal Schindler and von Breuning distributed funeral notices at Haslinger's music shop. The funeral took place at three o'clock on the afternoon of March 29.

The weather was fine. Twenty thousand people assembled. The schools of Vienna were closed and soldiers were called into the streets to preserve order. The pallbearers had difficulty in getting the coffin through the crowds. At one point in the procession from the church to the cemetery, the funeral march from his piano sonata, Op. 26, was played. Shubert, Hummel, Seyfried, Kreutzer and Czerny were among the thirty-eight torch bearers who followed the coffin.

At the cemetery, beside the open grave, the actor Anschutz delivered an oration, ending with the following lines: "He withdrew from men after he had given them everything and received nothing in return. He remained solitary . . . But even unto his grave he preserved a human heart for all who are human. . . . Thus he lived, thus he died, and thus he shall live forever."

Then in silence the coffin was lowered into its grave.

After the funeral Schubert and some friends went to a tavern and drank wine. Schubert raised his glass and proposed a toast. "To the one we have just buried!" All drank in silence. Then, filling his glass again, he added, "And to him who will be the next." He drank to himself, not knowing that he would be the next. He died in the fall of the following year.

The conversation books which Beethoven kept during the last eight years of his life, and which provide us with much information, fell into Schindler's hands. He destroyed some, for reasons which we do not know, and he sold the remaining one hundred and thirty-seven books to the Berlin library.

When the news of Beethoven's death reached England, the London *Times* wrote: "The loss to the musical world is irreparable, and will be heard with universal regret." A week or so later a letter was published in the *Times*, expressing surprise that "the Emperor of Austria, who professes to be such a patron of music, could have allowed this accomplished veteran to linger in misery" without coming to his aid.

The feeling of indignation was general in England, for in recording the funeral the *Times* added an editorial comment: "The file of carriages at the funeral of Beethoven, at Vienna, was said to be endless. A little more attention to him on the part of the owners, while living, would have been more to the purpose."

The £100 sent by the London Philharmonic Society was found untouched, by Beethoven's friends. Some of this money was used to pay for the funeral expenses and with great generosity the Society wrote that "in honor of the great deceased" the balance might go to the nephew Karl.

Karl also inherited the bank shares and everything else. The entire estate would have a value today of about $15,000. But this of course does not include the four precious instruments made by Amati and Guarnieri. These four instruments would now have a value of perhaps a half million dollars. About twenty years after Beethoven's death, Karl inherited about $90,000 from his uncle Johann.

Karl died in 1858, leaving a widow and several children. Thus was the name Beethoven carried forward. But the family sank lower and lower in the social scale. The last Beethoven was a simple, uneducated soldier who served in the Austrian army during World War I and who died in an army hospital in 1918.

About thirty-six years after Beethoven died, the Vienna Friends of Music Society had the body exhumed and re-buried in a better plot. Then in 1888, or sixty-one years after his death, his body was again moved by the Viennese people to a composers' Olympus, and here he was laid to his final rest beside the tombs of Mozart, Gluck and Schubert. Later two more joined this pantheon of music: Hugo Wolfe and Brahms.

To mark the place of Beethoven's grave a stone obelisk was erected. And on this stone a single word was carved: Beethoven.

SELECTED BIBLIOGRAPHY

Beethoven, Ludwig van. *Letters, Journals and Conversations*. Edited, translated and introduced by Michael Hamburger. New York: Pantheon Books Inc., 1952.

Burk, John N. *The Life and Works of Beethoven*. New York: Random House, Inc., 1943.

Crowest, Frederick J. *Beethoven*. London: Dent & Sons, 1899.

D'Indy, Vincent. *Beethoven: A Critical Biography*. Translated from the French by Theodore Baker. Boston: The Boston Music Co., 1911.

Newman, Ernest. *The Unconscious Beethoven; An Essay in Musical Psychology*. New York: Alfred A. Knopf, Inc., 1927.

Pryce-Jones, Alan. *Beethoven*. London: Duckworth, 1933.

Rolland, Romain. *Beethoven the Creator*. Translated by Ernest Newman. New York: Harper & Bros., 1929.

Schauffler, Robert Haven. *Beethoven: The Man Who Freed Music*. 2 vols. Garden City, N.Y.: Doubleday, Doran. 1929. Condensed edition in one vol. New York: Tudor Publishing Co., 1955.

Scott, Marion M. *Beethoven*. London: Dent & Sons, 1934.

Sullivan, John W. N. *Beethoven: His Spiritual Development*. New York: Alfred A. Knopf, Inc., 1927.

Thayer, Alexander W. *Life of Ludwig van Beethoven*. Edited and revised by Henry E. Krehbiel. 3 vols. Boston: E. C. Schirmer Music Co., 1921.

Wagner, Richard. *Beethoven*. Translated by A. R. Parsons. G. Schirmer, 1883.

SELECTED LIST OF BEETHOVEN
MUSIC AND RECORDINGS

SYMPHONIES

No. 3 "Eroica," Op. 55
No. 5 In C minor, Op. 67
No. 6 "Pastoral," Op. 68
No. 7 In A, Op. 92
No. 9 "Choral," Op. 125
   Splendid recordings of all nine symphonies have been
   made by Toscanini (RCA Victor); and by Bruno Walter
   (Columbia).

OVERTURES

Egmont, Op. 84
   Fine recordings of this composition have been made by
   Münch (Victor); Fritz Reiner (Victor); Walter (Colum-
   bia); and Toscanini (Victor).
Leonore, Op. 72, 72A, and 138
   Records by Toscanini (Victor) and Walter (Columbia)
   are outstanding.

[175]

PIANO CONCERTOS

No. 1 Op. 15
No. 2 Op. 19
No. 3 Op. 37
No. 4 Op. 58
No. 5 "Emperor," Op. 73
Many fine pianists have made brilliant recordings of Beethoven's concertos: Schnabel, Rubenstein, Gieseking, Backhaus, Serkin, Casadesus and others. The choice would be one of musical taste. Certainly Schnabel is the most scholarly, though dry, and Gieseking the most poetic. Each has its pianistic virtues.

CONCERTO IN D FOR VIOLIN, OP. 61

The world's greatest violinists have made wonderful recordings of this concerto, the only concerto Beethoven wrote for the violin. The outstanding performances are by Szigeti, Francescatti, Heifetz, Menuhin, Milstein, Oistrakh and Stern.

PIANO SONATAS

No. 8 *Pathétique,* Op. 13
Backhaus, Gieseking and Rubinstein have made fine recordings of this sonata.
No. 12 "Funeral March" Op. 26
Backhaus and Gieseking.
No. 14 "Moonlight," Op. 27, No. 2
Serkin, Horowitz, Backhaus.
No. 15 "Pastoral," Op. 28
Backhaus and Gieseking.
No. 17 "Tempest," Op. 31, No. 2
Backhaus, Badura-Skoda, Gieseking.
No. 21 "Waldstein," Op. 53
Horowitz, Rubinstein, Serkin.

No. 23 *Appassionata,* Op. 57
   Gieseking, Horowitz, Petri, Rubinstein, Serkin and Richter-Haaser.
No. 26 *Les Adieux,* Op. 81A
   Backhaus and R. Casadesus.
No. 29 "Hammerklavier," Op. 106
   No pianist has succeeded in making a convincing recording of this long and stormy sonata. But attempts were made by Backhaus, Petri, Kempff and others.
No. 30 Op. 109
   Backhaus, Gieseking, Gould and Serkin.
No. 31 Op. 110
   Backhaus, Gieseking and Richter-Haaser.
No. 32 Op. 111
   Backhaus, Gieseking, Gould and Richter-Haaser.

VIOLIN SONATAS

No. 1 Op. 12, No. 1
No. 2 Op. 12, No. 2
   The Heifetz recordings of both No. 1 and No. 2 are outstanding.
No. 5 "Spring," Op. 24
   Heifetz, Milstein and Oistrakh.
No. 9 "Kreutzer," Op. 47
   Francescatti, Milstein and Oistrakh.

TRIOS FOR PIANO, VIOLIN AND CELLO

No. 4 "Geister," Op. 70, No. 1
No. 6 "Archduke," Op. 97
   Of this very famous trio there are a number of fine recordings, one which was made by Rubinstein, Heifetz and Feuermann (Victor).

QUARTETS

Of Beethoven's sixteen quartets ten are especially famous and much loved. The last five quartets contain the most profound music ever written.

No. 7 "First Razoumowsky," Op. 59, No. 1
No. 8 "Second Razoumowsky," Op. 59, No. 2
No. 9 "Third Razoumowsky," Op. 59, No. 3
No. 10 "Harp," Op. 74
No. 11 "Serious," Op. 95
No. 12 Op. 127

This is the first of the famous "last five."

No. 13 Op. 130
No. 14 Op. 131

The quartet in C-sharp Minor which Beethoven himself as well as many others have considered to be the greatest of all.

No. 15 Op. 132
No. 16 Op. 135

A number of fine recordings of some of the quartets have been made by the Pascal Quartet. The complete sixteen have been recorded by the Budapest Quartet (Columbia) and the Hungarian Quartet (Angel). Both are fine, although the recordings by the Budapest group have achieved greater acclaim and reputation.

CHORAL

Mass in C, Op. 86

Beecham has made a fine recording (Capitol) of this bold and original work.

Missa Solemnis in D, Op. 123

Both Toscanini and Otto Klemperer have made excellent recordings of this most mystical of Beethoven's works.

INDEX

Adelaide, 55
Albrechtsberger, Johann Georg, 37
Alexander, Czar of Russia, 123
Amati violin, 61, 170
Amende, Karl, 53
American Revolution, 43, 112
Anschutz (actor), 169
Appassinoata Sonata (No. 23), 37, 43, 70, 72, 140
Apocrypha, The, 94

Bacchus, 139, 156
Bach, Johann Sebastian, 4, 14, 35, 56, 144
Bach, Karl Philipp Emanuel, 4, 13, 14, 36, 39, 56
Baden, 135
Battle Symphony, 121, 122, 123, 124. See also Wellington's Victory.
Beethoven, Johann (father of composer), 5, 6, 7, 9, 10, 11, 12, 33, 34
Beethoven, Johann (brother), 7, 11, 22, 34, 96, 115, 116, 159, 160, 170
Beethoven, Karl (brother), 7, 11, 22, 34, 116, 125
Beethoven, Karl (nephew), 125-138, 151, 159, 160, 161, 164, 167, 168, 170

Beethoven, Ludwig van (grandfather of composer), 4, 5, 7
Beethoven, Ludwig van, birth, 1, 4, 7; poverty, 8; early instruction, 9; beaten by father, 10; school, 11; first concert, 11; description of, 12; plays Bach; assistant organist, 15; first compositions, 15; appointment, 17; visit to Vienna, 18; sees Mozart, 19; on death of mother, 21; becomes head of family, 22; style of playing, 25; arrives in Vienna, 27; fame in England, 28; lives in palace, 32; death of father, 33, 34; lessons with Haydn, 36; as pianist, 38; method of teaching, 38, 39; effect on listeners, 40; friendship with the Brunswicks, 42; deafness, 44, 52-55; romance, 46; "Immortal Beloved" letter, 47-49; the "Heiligenstadt Testament," 49, 59-62; fondness for women, 50; "poet of melancholy," 55; musical influences, 56; Eroica, 65-68; his Second Period, 68; composes masterpieces, 69-83; quartets for Count Razoumowsky, 73-74; first performance of Fidelio, 81-83;

Beethoven, Ludwig van (*cont.*)
method of work, 84; description of,
89; his disorderly rooms, 92, 93;
handwriting, 98, 99; King of Westphalia offers him post of *Kapellmeister*, 101; meets Bettina Brentano and Goethe, 103-113; the
Mälzel association, 119-122; Congress of Vienna, 123-125; last appearance as pianist, 124; death of
brother, 125; guardianship of
nephew Karl, 125-137; third
period, 128; litigation, 133; Karl
attempts suicide, 135-137; agrees
to write two symphonies, 9th and
10th for Philharmonic Society of
London, 139; *Mass in D*, 143-145;
Choral Symphony, 145-148; com-
pletes last piano sonatas, 148-149;
last five quartets, 149-154; religion
of, 154-158; visits brother with his
nephew, 159-161; last illness, 161-
168; death, 169; funeral, 169-170;
final grave, 171
Beethoven, Maria (grandmother of
composer), 5
Beethoven, Maria Magdalena Laym
(mother of composer), 6, 7
Beethoven, Therese (Obermeyer),
(wife of Johann), 115, 116, 160,
165, 168
Bekker, Paul, 106
Berlioz, Hector, 56, 67, 78, 126
Bernadotte (French general), 64
Bibliography, 173
Bonaparte, Jerome (King of West-
phalia), 101, 102
Bonaparte, Joseph, 120
Bonaparte, Napoleon, 1, 2, 28, 29,
64, 65, 66, 81, 93, 102, 111, 112,
115, 117, 119, 120, 121 123, 125
Bonn, 4, 12, 13, 16, 21, 23, 25, 26,
27, 33, 34, 37, 43, 50
Brahms, Johannes, 56, 171
Brentano, Bettina, 49, 103-111
Breuning, Eleonora von, 23, 24, 33,
35
Breuning, Gerhard von, 162
Breuning, Lorenz von, 33

Breuning, Madame von, 23, 24, 90,
162, 165
Breuning, Stephan von, 24, 33, 98,
162, 165, 167, 168, 169
Bridgetower, George Augustus Pol-
green, 63
Broadwood piano, 118
Brunswick, Count von, 32, 43, 45
Brunswick, Countess Charlotte von,
43, 45
Brunswick, Countess Josephine von,
42, 44, 45, 49
Brunswick, Countess Therese von,
42, 43, 44, 45, 49
Brunswick, Franz von, 43
Bülow, Hans, 141
Burk, John N., 37, 55, 70, 73, 75,
127, 140, 141, 152
Byron, George Gordon, 113

C Minor Symphony. *See* Symphony
No. 5.
Caesar, 112
Cassel, Court of, 101, 102
Cecilia Society, 145
Choral Symphony. See Symphony
No. 9.
Clementi, Muzio, 34, 118
Coblenz, 28
Cologne, 11, 12, 16
Congress of Vienna, 2, 5, 29, 112,
123
Coriolanus Overture, 71
Corsica, 64
Czerny, Karl, 14, 38, 39, 40, 52, 64,
73, 75, 87, 88, 91, 98, 134, 140,
147, 169

Danube, 159, 160
Darmstadt, 85
Diabelli, Antonio, 164

Egmont, 108, 109, 110, 113, 157
Egypt, 155
Einstein, Alfred, 56, 67, 153
Elba, 112, 123, 125
Elector of Cologne, 4, 5, 6, 15, 16,
17, 18, 19, 22, 24, 25, 26, 27, 31,
34

Emperor Concerto (No. 5), 71, 74, 75
Empress of Russia, 124
Erdödy, Countess Marie von, 102
Erlkönig, 145
Eroica (Symphony No. 3), 2, 28, 32, 37, 65-68, 70, 71, 72, 76, 83, 88, 101, 111, 123, 146
Ertmann, Baroness Dorothea von, 32

Faust, 94, 95, 157
Ferdinand, Ruler of Modena, 16
Fidelio, 18, 71, 76, 80, 81, 95, 123
Franciscan monastery, 12
French Academy of Science, 113
French Revolution, 1, 3, 29, 34, 64, 112

Galitzin, Prince, 145, 149, 153
Gallenberg, Count, 46
Gelinek, Joseph, 35
Gluck, C. W., 89, 171
Gneizendorf, 160
Goethe, J. W. von, 94, 103-113, 145
Greece, 113
Greek mythology, 155
Guarnieri violin, 61, 170
Guicciardi, Countess Guilietta, 43, 45, 46, 49, 57

Hamburger, Michael, 92
Hammerklavier Sonata, No. 29. (Op. 106), 119, 138, 140, 141, 142, 148, 153
Handel, G. F., 4, 144, 163
Hapsburgs, 30
Harp Quartet, 71, 83
Haslinger's music shop, 169
Haydn, Franz Joseph, 4, 11, 26, 33, 36, 37, 56, 89, 101, 118, 164
Hayward, 110
Heiligenstadt, 58, 123
Heiligenstadt Testament, 49, 59-62, 123
Homer, 24, 94
Hummel, Johann N., 33, 96, 98, 164, 167, 169
Hüttenbrenner, Anselm, 168

Indy, Vincent D', 36, 50, 56, 145, 154
"Immortal Beloved," 46-49, 51

Joseph II, Emperor of Austria, 19, 29
Jahn, Otto, 19, 20

Karlsbad, 107
King of Prussia, 148
Kinsky, Prince Ferdinand, 102, 117, 122
Klopstock, 94
Koch, Babette, 50
Koch, Friar Willibald, 12
Kreutzer, Rudolph, 63, 169
Kreutzer Violin Sonata, 63, 64
Krumpholz, Wenzel, 64, 68

Last five quartets, Nos. 12 to 16, 149-154
Last Sonata, No. 32, 149
Leonora, 80-81 (See *Fidelio*)
Leonora overture, 18
Leopold II of Austria, 29
Lichnowsky, Prince Karl, 32, 33, 61, 91
Lichnowsky, Princess, 72, 82
Linz, 96, 115, 126, 160
Liszt, Franz, 14, 56
Lobkowitz, Prince, 32, 66, 67, 102, 117, 122
Louis Ferdinand, Prince of Prussia, 66

Macbeth, 77, 95, 157
Magic Flute, The, 80
Malfatti, Dr., 165
Mälzel, Johann N., 119-122
Marie Antoinette, 1, 4, 16, 26, 29
Marie Caroline, Queen of Naples, 16
Maria Theresa, Empress of Austria, 16, 19
Mass in D (See *Missa Solemnis*)
Matthison (poet), 97
Maximilian, Franz, Archduke (Elector of Cologne), 16
Mendelssohn, Felix, 113
Missa Solemnis in D, 18, 133, 138, 139, 143, 144, 145, 146, 150, 154

Moonlight Sonata (No. 14), 55, 57, 70
Moscheles, Ignaz, 166, 167
Mount of Olives, The, 63
Mozart, W. A., 4, 10, 12, 13, 14, 19, 20, 25, 29, 30, 31, 32, 33, 37, 38, 39, 56, 80, 84, 89, 96, 101, 118, 171

Neate, Charles, 85
Neefe, Christian Gottlob, 13, 14, 15, 18
Newman, Ernest, 40

Obermeyer, Therese (wife of Johann). *See* Beethoven, Therese
Olympus, 155, 162, 171
Oriental philosophy, 94

Paganini, Nicolò, 10
Pastoral Sonata (No. 15), 70
Pathétique Sonata, 55
Patterson, Elizabeth, 102
Peters, Carl (music publisher), 133
Peters, Councilor, 133
Pfeiffer, Tobias, 12
Philharmonic Society of London, 97, 139, 145, 148, 163, 166, 170
Piano Concerto No. 3, 63
Piano Concerto No. 4, 71, 74, 83
Piano Concerto No. 5, (*Emperor*), 71, 74, 75, 83, 88

Radziwill, Prince, 145
Razoumowsky, Count Andreas, 32, 72, 124
Razoumowsky Quartets, 32, 71, 72, 95, 124
Reiche, Anton, 33
Rhine, 27, 91, 160
Ries, Ferdinand, 37, 50, 58, 65, 90, 139
Ritterballet music, 25
Rolland, Romain, 49, 68, 89, 106
Rudolph, Archduke, 75, 102, 117, 124, 133, 139

St. Petersburg, 150

Salieri, Antonio, 37
Schauffler, Robert, 67, 73, 86, 106, 109, 140, 142, 143
Schiller, Friedrich, 94, 118, 146, 147, 155
Schindler, Anton, 18, 49, 83, 98, 149, 164, 165, 167, 168, 169 170
Schlemmer, 135
Schlösser Louis, 85
Schmidt, Dr., 58, 59
Schnabel, Artur, 140
Schubert, Franz, 84, 85, 145, 163, 164, 169, 171
Scott, Marion M., 49, 146
Sebald, Amalie, 49
Selected List of Beethoven Music and Recordings, 175-178
Seyfried, Ignaz von, 169
Shakespeare, 80, 94, 112
Smetana (surgeon), 135
Sorrows of Werther, The, 108, 112
Spohr, Louis, 117
Streicher, Andreas, 118
Streicher, Madame Nanette, 117, 118, 119
Stein, Johann Andreas, 118
Stravinsky, Igor, 56
Stumpff, Johann, 163
Sturm und Drang, 108
Sullivan, J. W. N., 68, 73, 75, 77, 106, 128, 140, 141, 146, 147
Symphony No. 2, 62, 69
Symphony No. 3. *See Eroica*
Symphony No. 4, 69, 83
Symphony No. 5, 69, 71, 76, 78, 83, 88, 95, 101, 113
Symphony No. 6 (*Pastoral*), 69, 76, 79, 83, 88, 95
Symphony No. 7, 115, 121, 124, 126
Symphony No. 8, 115, 116, 121, 126, 144
Symphony No. 9 (*Choral Symphony*), 139, 143, 144, 145, 147, 152
Symphony No. 10, 139, 167

Thayer, Alexander W., 12, 49, 71, 106
Trémont, Baron de, 92

Van den Eeden (organist), 12, 13
Vienna, 18, 20, 26, 27, 30, 40, 44,
    45, 50, 58, 61, 67, 72, 81, 83, 85,
    87, 88, 90, 93, 101, 102, 116, 121,
    123, 124, 135, 136, 148, 159, 160,
    161, 164, 170
Vienna Friends of Music Society, 171
Vienna Opera House, 81, 83
Violin Concerto, 71, 74, 76, 83, 88

Wagner, Richard, 56, 126
Waldstein, Count Ferdinand, 25, 26,
    31

Waldstein Sonata (No. 21), 26, 37,
    70, 72
Weber, Karl Maria von, 150
Wegeler, Franz Gerhard, 24, 27, 33,
    46, 53, 57, 91
Wellington's Victory, 28, 120. See
    also *Battle Symphony.*
Westphalia, King of, 101
Wolfe, Hugo, 171
Württemberg, King of, 102

Zenser (organist), 12
Zeuner (viola player), 150
Zmeskall, Nicolaus, 64